Fantasies, Imagining and Memories.

Chin'er

Photos by Pu-Chin
Illustration by Zoe Waide

WORKBOOK PRESS LLC
187 E Warm Springs Rd
Suite B285 Las Vegas NV 89119 USA

Website: https://workbookpress.com/
Hotline: 1-888-818-4856
Email: admin@workbookpress.com

Ordering Information:
Quantity sales. Special discounts are available on quantity purchases by corporations, associations, and others. For details, contact the publisher at the address above.

ISBN-13: 978-1-965732-61-8 Paperback Version
        978-1-965732-62-5 Digital Version
        978-1-965732-63-2 Hardcover Version

REV. DATE: 08/25/2025

Fantasies, Dreams and Memories

Frankincense and myrrh, have I not,
Nor jewels nor gold in my pithy lot,
Neither furs nor fancy velvet garb,
Nor rich foods nor fattening carbs,
Do I dare share or give to you?
My friends, a story or two, which my life
Did change, probably 'til the bitter end.

Contents

A Handfull Of Rice 1

What's in a Name 8

Chicken-neck Soup 13

Perfect Crime and Freedom 19

From before the beginning to after the end 49

HLASSA 54

Hurricane Surfing 97

Nature against Nature – the STORM 107

Night Vs Day 122

Dawu_One Hundred Years Later 135

The Last Rendezvous 144

Two Minutes 166

About the Author 170

A Handfull Of Rice

All the girls in school were terribly excited as it was the last day of school and all our trunks were packed and been 'coollied' (carried on the heads of porters) down to the railway station. We were excited because we were going home for our Winter holidays after being away for nine months, but also, we felt a bit sad because we will not see our friends for three months, since many of us came from other parts of the country, even other countries. As we milled about the assembly hall, we waited for our names to be called, then filed out in pairs, always in pairs as we were always told. When everyone was filed behind our school gates, the Mother Superior came to give us a final 'farewell' talk – always the same, "Be good girls, love your parents and family, try to read all your book assignments, help your younger brothers and sisters, and most of all don't forget to say your prayers before you go to bed, we will be praying for you." We shifted about on our feet, impatient and bored, why do they always have to repeat themselves. The gate was finally opened, we would have preferred to rush out and run down to the station, but like well brought up little girls, we filed out behind the Prefects, and were able to go only as fast as they walked. No pushing, no shoving, no shouting. At that time, I was already taller than most of my school-mates and my strides were longer, and it was quite a few years later that I was at the front of the file and was able to have my revenge. By then I was the tallest girl in school and the fastest walker, and by walking my normal speed, my partner and I were soon far ahead of the rest of the column. I remember once, the nuns in the back had to send up a runner to tell me to slow down. It was a satisfying moment.

Anyway, to recapitulate, we filed out and slowly walked out of the school grounds to the station. Along the way, the shop keepers came out and stood at their respective doorways and cheered and waved "bye-bye' to us. We grinned and waved back, shouting, "See you in March." We arrived at the small Toy Train Station where the station Master was waiting for us. Our school had commandeered the entire little train. I did not realize at that time that this was to be a truly Historic Moment. Our DHR–Darjeeling Himalayan Railways–was to become famous one day. But that year it was still OUR dirty, snail paced little

Toy Train which we all loved dearly. It was so slow going around the curves and bends of the mountain tracks that some of us could jump out and scamper down the hillside, meet it further down the tracks and hop back on. During one short, 'straightish' section, which were far and few between, we met the local postman on his bicycle, the train gave a hoot, the postman raised his arm and the race was on! We girls cheered our engine driver and stuck out our tongues at the postman as we barely overtook him. As we came down the mountain side and the terrain leveled out, the heat became unbearable, we were used to the cool perpetual Spring temperatures of seven thousand feet. Finally, we arrived at the REAL train station in Siliguri, where we had to change into a full sized three-meter wide train. The entire train had been taken over by us school girls. Very soon, our nuns had very efficiently installed us into our own compartments – eight girls in each. This was our last time, for three months, when we can spend time with our best friends. These trips are worth another story.

It was an over-night trip From Siliguri to Sealda Station in Calcutta, now Kolkata, but I don't think any of the older girls slept, they seem to have endless things to say to each other. We younger ones slept soundly till we were wakened by the call of "Breakfast, 'yegges, tos, tea......"(eggs, toast, tea) all sounded yummy. We climbed out of our 'holdalls,' bed-rolls, rather like a canvas sleeping bag without zips, into which contained our flattened quilt, pillow and our pajamas (an Indian word, by the way) We jumped down from our upper bunks. The bearer, of breakfast, came in with trays of food. Most of us were ravenous after all the excitement and long train trip down the mountain. The was to be one of several meals brought to us by the bearer. The weather became hotter and hotter as we came down to the plains and the huge tea plantations were replaced by small and large agricultural plots of varieties of vegetables, and interspersed here and there, often, very close to each other were tall mango trees with dark green canopies of shiny green leafy branches. I can just imagine when they are covered with ripe golden mangoes – what a king's feast they must present to all the children, green parrots and monkeys all around.

At noon, the bearer came with our lunches of chappaties, an unleavened flat bread made of stone-ground wheat flour, chicken or vegetable curries, dhal (lentil curry) and bananas. After that we were told to take a nap, whether we were tired or not. Since we had been awakened very early the previous morning, most of us younger ones did nap. But it seemed we had just fallen into deep slumber, when the bearer of nourishment called out again, "chai (sweet milk-tea), biscoot,(cookies), jam-tos" and wonders galore, "samosa," a pyramid shaped ravioli filled with vegetable curry, and deep fried, quite scrumptious. We rubbed our eyes and went to them. This was tea-time, so we must be nearing Calcutta, the landscape had changed even further, the garden plots were smaller and the water-tanks also smaller and seemed a good deal dirtier, often taking on a slimy green tinge – not unlike those "green health drinks" for which unsuspecting health obsessed people pay good money for in our "land of milk and honey!'

Now fully awake we were anxiously waiting for our arrival at Sealda. But there was one more meal to be had – dinner. It was the last thing in our minds, but the familiar cry came down the corridor, "Dinner! Rice, mutton curry, dhal, ice-Scream."

"Wow," we screamed, "Ice scream." When the trays were put in front of us, every girl, in spite of the nuns' and prefects', warnings of doom, first dove into their tiny cardboard cups of delicious vanilla ice-cream. By then I had had too much food already, but I carefully wrapped up my rice and vegetable curry in the cardboard container, poured the dhal into the ice cream cup and wrapped everything up carefully in my nice white handkerchief, which we all had to have as part of our uniform.

Gathering our belongings, we searched for our families on the crowded platform. It was miraculous that somehow bags and baggage found their rightful owners since each lot was piled onto the heads of porters already dashing out of the station. We girls ran into the waiting arms of our families and immediately turned to follow the porters, or we would never see our luggage again.

The platform widened into a vast pillared common waiting area at the entrance, which doubled as a shelter for the homeless. At the base of each pillar which provided a slightly more comfortable space, lodged a family and their ill and elderly, who could lean against the pillars and rest easier. No one saw nor cared about them. As I walked by such an 'inhabited' pillar, I noticed a family of thirteen gathered at its base. They were all focused on the oldest member of the family. The patriarch, clad in a rough gunnysack shirt over long paper-thin loin-cloth, had in the palms of his hands a wide banana leaf filled with faintly colored yellow rice, probably someone's discarded lunch. A young woman in a thin, grey cotton sari bent over the old man and began to share tiny scoops of rice with each member of the family. Hungry eyes, especially of the little ones, followed the woman's fingers in case a grain or two might fall to the ground.

I thought guiltily of my own unfinished food in my handkerchief and went up to the old man and emptied it onto his banana leaf – a small addition to his family of thirteen. The family looked up at me and nodded, the children grinned with the anticipation of getting more than a few grains of yellow rice that day. I slowly walked passed them and found my own family waiting at our car.

Come Christmas every year, and I am confronted with a table overladen with an impossibly abundance of food, most of which may be uneaten or discarded, I think of that family and their little grains of yellow rice and watery dhal stew.

What's in a Name

"**O**h Darling, I think the baby is coming, you had better take me to the hospital." Her husband's mouth dropped, though he had been waiting for these very words for almost a month now, but still it was both a dreaded and exhilarating moment.

"My goodness, what is the name of the hospital, and where is it? Where did I put my address book, I cannot seem to remember anything, darling, do you know in what safe place I had kept it?" He rummaged around his desk, her desk, the bedside table, in the bathroom......." And getting into a panic he twirled around the room in despair.

"Darling, I am sure you put in into your overcoat pocket."

"Ah yes, of course I did. I had wanted to be sure it was with me when I drove to the hospital."

Carefully, and holding his wife gingerly, they slipped out into the silent and secretive night to the hospital. With extreme and unnecessary care, he helped his wife into the front seat of their car.

"Oh dear, will she fit into the seat, she looks much too big, what will I do if she will not," he thought to himself. "There is no time to call for a van- cab. Pray God, she will fit." Very gingerly he took his wife's left arm over his shoulders.

"Honey, there is really no need to do that, I can manage, see," she quicly slid into the seat. Then he took the seat belt and reached over her large belly to clip it on.

"Oh my, I'm going to crush the baby," he thought. The wife took the end of the seat belt and efficient and easily clicked into place.

"Darling, don't worry, I am alright, I can manage, please lets go to the hospital now, before it is too late." She said, trying to not alarm further. But the poor man was so agitated that it took him a while to fumble about trying to put the seat belt over his wife's big belly, afraid he might hurt the baby or her, or......... panic struck again. He then looked for his car keys and could not find it in any of his pockets.

"It is in the ignition already, darling, you put it in as soon as we came to the car."

"Ah yes, how stupid of me, of course I did. I don't know what has come over me, can't seem to do anything, nor think clearly. We must get going."

So saying, he got in the car, put is it in reverse, and backed out of the driveway and sped down the road. As soon as they arrived, a nurse was waiting outside with a wheel chair and took charge. The husband was told to sit in the waiting room, relax and wait. He sat down, got up and walked around the room, sat down again, picked up a magazine, flipped through the pages without seeing anything and put it down and picked up another one; he went through all the magazines in the rack then sat down and fidgeted about. Finally it dawned on him that he should probably phone his and her immediate families and tell them to be expectant too. The questions were too numerous and came at him too fast to respond. He was all in a whirl and said the most meaningful thing, "I don't know." Then the nurse came and told him he could to go his wife as she is not yet ready to deliver. He went into his wife's room, and in his eagerness almost knocked over the bedside table. He hugged his wife, sat down beside the bed and held her hand, not knowing what to say.

"I have phoned Mom and your mother too and some of the others." But before he could finish the first of the relatives began to arrive.

After an hour or so, the nurses told everyone to come out to the waiting room and relax. They were not helpful in the delivery room. They came out to the waiting room and was confronted by all the other relatives – brothers, sisters, and all the senior in-laws – he was totally overwhelmed.

"What are you all doing here?" he almost screamed,

"You had said that you don't know anything, so we decided to come and see for ourselves," said the wife's mother's Alpha sister, "SO! what have you decided to call him?"

"What, we don't know whether......"

"You don't even know what you are going to call your son."

"No, no, I mean" again he was interrupted, this time by his own mother. "I thought we had decided to call him 'Nicolas' sweetheart."

"I do not like that name," objected the wife's father, "too monkish."

"How about, Alistair," chimed in the brother,

"Nay," said the sister, "people will not know how to spell or pronounce it, also it sounds too 'gay.'

"What about a simple name like Thomas, or John or Simon?" said another brother.

"Never, those names will be contracted into ghastly Johnny, or Tom or, some smart aleck will say "Simple Simon, met a Pieman..... Never those names for Chris' sake."

"I agree," chimed in another brother, "Tasteless names."

The poor father forlornly looked from one face to another, could not utter a single word.

"NOW," suddenly proclaimed the matriarch, "you should call him "Christopher" with a 'ph' not an f! That is the name I like. Yes that is what you must call him." The father shrugged and nodded weakly in compliance.

"I can't believe his weakness," stage whispered Alpha sister-in-law. "yes, yes, you are right, he is a bit of a weakling," agreed her husband.

This went on and on, the cacophony became louder and louder so that it seemed everyone was arguing and a fight was going to break out. Quietly, unnoticed by the arguing relatives, the father slipped out of the waiting room back to his wife. He looked into the delivery room anxiously, the doctor and his helpers were just cleaning the wee infant and putting the tiny pink skullcap and wrapping a baby blanket around the pink little bundle. A nurse brought it to him and announce:

"Congratulations, you have a beautiful baby girl."

Chicken-neck Soup

He came home one night, drunk as usual. Staggering and singing as he climbed up to his small but light-filled attic apartment. Here he was able to climb out of his window onto the roof and look out over the entire complex of variegated roofs. When he was sober, he would sit on his small rattan stool and watch what was going on: carefully and lovingly tended potted vegetables and flowers on the flat roofs, colorful clothing hanging out to dry, others with their small wooden stools around tables set with mahjong pieces. It was quite idyllic. He would not move to a more spacious apartment even if he could afford it. This night, people in other apartments told him to shut up as he noisily sang Beijing opera excerpts and stumbled up the concrete steps. Finally, reaching his apartment, fumbling for his keys, opened his living-dining room and fell in, barely upright. Straightaway, he went to the far end of the large room where he had all his "artist's accoutrement,"-his easel, work table with pots of paints, large brushes carefully planted in large tall jugs, brush side clean and upright, other smaller and more delicate ones were hanging on several brush- hangers. His large and most favorite inkstone along with the inksticks were artist waiting for him. He tottered about his room almost knocking down his easel and peered into his waste basket,

"Aha, you are in your bed as usual, eh?"

"Hey, hey," he chuckled, "This is your lucky day, my friend, you will be my supper tonight."

The snake, for that was his 'friend' had been living in his waste basket for many months, how it got there, he did not know, but it kept his apartment free of mice and other unwanted critters who loved to chew on his rice papers and expensive painting silks. The reptile was curled up on his newest painting of an advertisement for some new silk stocking that had been imported by the department store for which he was working, a job he did not like, he preferred to paint landscapes, bamboos and beautiful women, but he had a great thirst and hunger so he had to please his employer. He went into his little kitchen and took out a cleaver. The snake was still innocently curled up on the silk stocking picture, totally uninterested in what was going to happen to him. The knife came up and cleaved again and again till the poor animal was in numerous segments. He then set down his knife, sat on his artist's stool and wept, he had just killed his old friend simply because he was hungry and drunk. He wept for a long time, then sobering, he got up and wrapped the poor thing in the advertisement painting, cleaned up the blood and terrible mess and put the lot into the largest pot he owned.

"What am I going to do now? How will I cook this friend?" He wept again then remembered the 'old wives' tale' that snakes had to be cooked under the open sky, because if the soot from the kitchen ceiling fell into the pot, the poison will be extracted out of the snake and make the meal inedible. Then, very quietly, he went downstairs with his 'dinner,' to the communal kitchen which was open to a courtyard. Finding a large pot, he placed it on a pile of charcoal and started the fire. The artist sat and stoked his meal for several hours. He tasted the soup for seasoning and when he was satisfied, waited till the pot was cool enough to take upstairs. By the time he returned to his flat, it was almost daylight, but he was very pleased with himself and decided to invite his favorite friends to share his meal. He wrote out several invitations and slipped them under the doors of his friends. Finally, returning to his apartment, crawled into bed dreaming of a delicious and entertaining repast that was to happen.

He set the table for ten, in his living room, and admired his handiwork. Then he waited. Promptly at seven, the guests started to arrive. One by one they took their seats, among the guest was a five-year old girl with a mass of curly hair who often came up to his apartment to watch him paint.

"You like my paintings, little one." She nodded shly, without stopping to grind his inkstick on his beautiful stone which was shaped like a half-opened lotus leaf. He had taught her how to hold the inkstick lightly but firmly, put a small spoon of water on the stone and grind it steadily and smoothly in one circular direction until the water turned into a luminous deep black liquid. It was mesmerizing and satisfying, and she loved to do it then watch him perform with this liquid and his brushes his magic on the thin pieces of rice paper.

"AH, welcome everybody, tonight I have made a special soup to celebrate our friendship," of course he was really thinking of his friend, the snake, when he said this. He lifted the large pot in the center of the table, with a dramatic gesture and revealed the soup. His friends looked, eyebrows went up and questions poised on their lips...

"What kind of soup is this."

"Why is it so white?'

"Did you use milk?"

"Did you use tofu paste to make it so white?"

He simple chuckled and ladled out bowlfuls of the milky soup placing a bowl in front of each one. They spooned it and started to eat.

"This tastes rather good," said one guest, "What is the meat?"

"How long did you have to cook this, there seems to be a lot of bones," Said another.

"Of course, it is a bone soup," replied the artist, smiling sweetly.

"But I cannot find any real meat," complained a third.

Then all of a sudden, the little girl piped up and said, "Uncle, why did you use only chickon necks?" The guests looked at one another, and said, "Lao Chang is playing tricks on us again." At this point the little girl's mother got up, excused herself and hurriedly left.

"Ahya!" the artist exclaimed, "what's with all these questions, you said my soup tasted good, so eat it, shup up and be quiet. Eat!"

Rather rapidly, one by one, the guests left leaving only the little girl and her father, who was the artist's best friend.

"Ha, ha, ha." They laughed and slapped their thighs at the joke. "Those silly people, even afraid of chicken-neck-soup," said the artist.

"Alas, I lost a good friend, what will I do with the mice now?"

The three of them enjoyed the meal thoroughly, the little girl's father knew, but his daughter did not till she was well into her teens.

Perfect Crime and Freedom

Lamu had send their daughter to her mother's for the week-end saying that she had some extra work she had to complete for someone, and needed to have time on her own to do it. The truth of the matter was that since their daughter had turned seventeen four months ago, she was already showing signs of a budding beautiful young woman, she had also started to notice certain little unpleasant changes taking place in her fifty-two year old husband. Secret lecherous smiles aimed at Tara, a touch on the shoulder, an accidental brush pass or a slightly prolonged hug much too close to his own bosom, all made Lamu extremely uncomfortable. She herself had endured all manner of abuse, excesses and demands because she was his wife, his 'stupid ass,' his slave, his 'chain around his neck.' Etcetera, etcetera. She must not let their daughter suffer the same humiliations which would be far worse, a taboo and a mortal sin. She will put an end to his evil ruminations and deeds once and for all.

That week he had spent several days going back and forth to the border area to exchange goods, and on Friday night, he would be exhausted and angry as usual. He will come back drunk with the smell of tschang (local fermented-millet beer) and demand for her attention, except this time he did not call for her, he wanted Tara to wash and massage his feet after his long hours of driving. Tara trembled with fear but could not refuse. Her mother brought in a basin of hot water with herbs and put it down at his feet. Tara knelt beside it and took her father's feet, one at a time, and placed them in the scalding water.

"Ahya," the father yelled, "What are you doing, you donkey, are you trying to cook me?' He shouted. Tara cringed and looked up, terrified, as she had not been warned by her mother that she would put scalding water into the basin and will need some cold water to temper the heat.

"I'm so sorry, papa, so sorry. I should have felt it before I placed your feet in the hot water," but before she could finish, her father kicked her with his dry foot and tried to step out of the basin, but being totally drunk, instead, he stepped on the basin's rim towards himself and spilt the rest of the boiling water onto his own legs, which almost immediately burst into a mass of little boils.

"Oyo, oyo, oyo you little witch, I'll kill you, where is your stupid ugly mother, why is she not here to help, get her, you fool."

Tara rushed out of the room and almost ran into her mother who had arrived, cool and calm with a large towel draped over her left arm.

"Tara, go, run to grandma, and stay with her till I come for you." She whispered to her daughter. "Do not say anything to anyone, not even grandma. Just tell her I had something to take care of alone." Tara ran as fast as she could down the hill towards the hamlet near the stream.

Lamu came towards her moaning husband prostrate floor, covered with hot water and legs boiling with puss dribbling down onto the dirt floor. He groaned and in spite of his pain, he tried to grab a hold of Lamu and bring her down and strike her.

"I will strangle you, you ugly pig," he hissed. But she was too fast for the drunken, dissimulated man, managed to get around to the back of him and with one quick blow to his head with the wooden meat mallet she had hidden in the towel, she silenced him. Quietly and methodically, she put an end to her hated husband. After she had cleaned up the mess, put away the tools she had used for the job, and all was back to 'normal,' she then calmly lay down on the floor beside the bed, her usual place of slumber after her husband had had his fill of her. Oddly enough, she did fall into a sound and peaceful sleep, better than any sleep she had had since the first day she was brought to this man's house. Alas, she was rudely awakened by her husband's driving partner.

"Hey man, what happened to you, we are supposed to be at the "godown" (ware-house) half an hour ago, they will dock our salary for two hours if we don't get there now." The man pushed the door open and went into the bedroom. Privacy was not a word common here. He looked in and saw Lamu, on the floor, awakened, but her damn husband was still asleep.

"What's the matter with him?" He asked the wife, "we were supposed to be at work half an hour ago."

"I don't know," said Lamu, still filled with sleep, "He came home late and drunk as usual," he didn't even want his dinner and went straight to bed." Lamu got up and shook him,

"Wake up, sir, you are late for work," she said to her dead husband respectfully. One always has to show respect for one husband, especially in front of his colleagues. Of course, he did not wake up, she shook him harder, then "ayoma," she wailed, "he is cold, what has happened? What has happened to my husband," she feigned horror, sadness, terror, then she screamed with the realization that she had actually managed to kill her husband, who had tortured her since the first day she had married him – which had started with a terrifying rape, and never stopped.

She crumpled onto the floor and cried, more from relief that she had finally got rid of her torturer and saved her daughter from him, rather than that he was dead, but of course only she knew the truth. The neighbors came to comfort her, and others brought her food and drink. She was satisfied. The police could find no signs of any wrong doings, no break-ins, no thefts, no sign of any struggle; but the doctor was puzzled, true there was no sign of struggle, not even blood anywhere, but something was not totally right, the death was too sudden. The man was a nasty fellow, but he was sound of body whose heart seemed normal, because one automatically assumed heart failure when there is a sudden death. Of course, everyone in the town knew he was a wife-beating drunkard,

"Ah," thought the doctor, "perhaps he was

so drunk that he choked on his own vomit and suffocated himself." So, he pronounced him 'dead of suffocation." He had always felt deeply sorry for the man's wife, who never complained and had gone about her wife and family duties with quiet dignity. He had delivered their little girl and came to know her a little bit. There were times when he felt that she wanted to talk to him, but, was too fearful all the time. He too had wanted to talk to her, but, was always too shy to say anything. Now he went up to Lamu and said quietly, "If you should need any help of any kind, please come to me. I will help you." She looked at him like a scared little rabbit, nodded and managed a weak smile.

The neighbors and Lamu's friends notified her parents and daughter. Tara ran as fast as she could to be with her long suffering but steely mother and fell into her arms."

"Amma, Amma." She sobbed. I am so sorry, so afraid." They clung onto each other while the rest of the family and friends took care of everything, even the monks, who seem to know what is going on all the time, materialized from somewhere. They cleared and cleaned and chanted.

Everyone gathered around. During the ceremony for the dead, Lamu made herself as quiet and tragic a figure as she could, keeping always in the background, and tried to remember her life before she was forced into this crime, "Nay," she thought to herself, "Put an end to a lifelong crime against me." She was satisfied with her own judgement. She felt no guilt, just pure relief and perhaps an inkling of freedom at last.

Lamu had just started in her Std. 11 with one more year to finish High School. It was a simple school divided into four "schools" – Primary: from Kinder Garden, which was optional, Standard 1 to Standard 3; Middle: from Std. 4 to Std.7; Upper Middle: from Std. 8 to std.10 and finally Std. 11 and 12.

She was very excited at the prospect of finishing school and then get a job to earn some money to help her parents in their little flower shop they owned and had run even since she could walk. Kalimpong, situated in the Eastern Himalayas is about three and a half thousand feet above sea level. It is the major a trade and smugglers' stop-over between China, Tibet, Sikkim, Bhutan and India. Except for the annual downpour of Monsoon rains between June and September, the climate is almost perpetual Spring. The Winters are not severe, at least it never snowed and temperature hardly dipped below fourty degrees Fahrenheit. Most of its inhabaitants are Indians, Tibetans, Nepalese, Lopchu, and other Himalaya tribes. It is famous for her flowers and spices, especially gladioli and cardamom. Such products were shipped all over India and even as far as Australia and England. Her father ran their little flower and spice business, while her mother looked after four little ones at home. Luckily, they had room enough in their tiny three bed room apartment for her 'nani,' maternal grandmother to stay. At first, her father was not too pleased with the situation, wife and mother-in-law under one roof and sharing one kitchen was often not a good mix. But over the years, he saw how helpful she was to his wife, with the cooking, the cleaning and even the small change now and then to help with household expenses. She had even promised to sell some of her dowry jewelry when Lamu was ready to marry.

Alas that day came all too soon.

She was barely seventeen when they came for her, she had not even finished her high school.

"But Papa, I have only one more year when I will finish High School, then I will be able to help you and Amma in the shop." Lamu protested.

"Shut up and listen. We have found a very good man, slightly older than you. (In fact, he was twice her age). He has a job transporting goods back and forth between Kalimpong and the Tibetan boarder. He is well paid and has no other family to share in his wages."

"But, but, Papa, I really want to finish school, I am so close."

"He even owns the small house he lives in, it has a tiny garden in the back where you can grow your own vegetables. Most importantly, he does not demand any dowry, he just wants a woman to do some light cooking, keep his bed warm in Winter and keep his house clean and garden well tended. Sounds like a perfect find."

"Papa," Lamu interrupted, "I am doing very well in class, I have gotten good marks in all my grades, especially in 'Maths.' My teacher says that if I continue to do so well, maybe I will be able to get a scholarship and go to college in Darjeeling. They told me there is an especially good girls' school there, where even the princesses of Nepal send their daughters. You would be so proud of me when you see me in college."

Oh dear, this was the wrong thing to say.

"College, what college, go to college and

learn all those useless books when you could be married and bring up a family? What good is that." Her father was getting red in the face at the thought of his daughter sitting idly around reading books and eating ladoos and samosas (Indian snacks).

Lamu was dumbfounded, and before she could say another word, her father announced,

"You will not go to school tomorrow, I will go and see the Principal myself and tell him the good news." She was so furious, she too got red in the face, stamped her feet on the floor and ran into the bed room she shared with her three siblings, and sat on her bed and fumed, if there was something to throw she would have smashed it and thrown it out of the little window. She did have a temper and her siblings stayed clear from her when she was like that. Then the youngest little girl sidled up to her like a wee seductive kitten,

"Barrah Didi (big sister), please don't be so angry, you are scaring me because I don't understand why you are so red in the face," at this Lamu picked up her littlest sister, hugged her fiercely, tousled her hair and said,

"No Little One, I am not angry with you, only

I am angry with the world. We girls are treated so unfairly." Her other siblings, one girl of thirteen and a boy of ten, looked at her not understanding at all, except perhaps the thirteen-year old girl. "You see, Papa told me that I have to stop going to school and get married to an old man!" This made the blood rise into her face again.

"But you love school," said Dolma, the thirteen-year old, "and you always told me to study hard and finish school, and that it was the most important thing to do in life. Does not our father agree with that?" She was really puzzled.

"Yes, it is the most important thing to do in life, but not for girls. For us the most important thing to do, it seems to the adults, is to get married and have babies and start and a family."

"Eeeyu," chimed in Kancha, the ten-year old boy, "Yuk,"

"Shut up," scolded Dolma, "what do you know, stupid boy, and you will get all the advantages in life." Now she was getting red in the face too. She also had a bit of a temper, but not as fiery as her older sister, and seldom roused.

"Ahya, Dolma, let him be," said Lamu,

"But it is so unfair," cried Dolma, "I understand

just what you are saying, the boys in the class can talk back at the teacher, thrown paper darts in the classes, the teachers just smile, as if with approval! While we girls can only sit quietly and recite the lessons. It is so unfair, so unfair. Makes me want to throw up!"

"Well, my wise little sister, you are just seeing the beginning. Be strong and learn how to 'tsr koo' (eat bitter, a Chinese saying). One day we will be equal with the boys. Just wait and see."

Next morning Mr. Tshering, the father put on his cleanest Tibetan gown and walked down to the Government school. It was a simple but large school, and the playground was already a loud and confused gathering of boys and girls of all ages and sizes in white shirts and dark blue trousers or skirts, matching blue ties were hung skewed dangerously around innocent slender necks. There were no balls to kick or throw, so stones, dirt balls or paper darts flew around, or some children even kicked up piles of dirt mounds just for fun. Mr. Tshering gingerly wound around all this confusion and after many queries he found the principal's office, which overlooked the play-ground. Sitting behind a large ancient wooden desk was a grey-haired man in a crumpled suit studying some papers strewn across his desk top.

He looked up, smiled and said, "Good morning Mr. err....."

"Tshering, Sir," replied respectfully, "My name is Tshering, and I am the father of Lamu in your Std. 11."

"Ah yes," the smile grew wider and with a kindly nod said, "Do sit down Mr. Tshering, we know Lamu well, she is the pride and joy of her class and of the entire school, every child seems to know her, and she has a smile or encouraging word for everyone. Can I help you?"

"Err," Tshering hesitated, after such an opening, how can he put what he was going to tell the Principal? "Yes, I have come to talk about Lamu." he looked down at his feet, then at the desk and finally at the Principal himself. "You see, Mr. Principal, Lamu is more than more than seventeen now, she is of age......" the Principal began to frown, he suspected what was coming, as he has had several similar 'interviews' before, but he wanted the father to squirm and sweat and suffer through what he was about to say, he had no sympathy for such parents.

"Yes, go on," he prompted, his earlier

welcoming smile changed to a stern and intimidating countenance.

"Lamu is seventeen now, and... hmmmmm.... it is time for her to share in the responsibilities in the house. We need her at home," Tshering tried to beat around.

"Yes, please go on, I do not have much time, and as you can hear, the noise is getting louder on the playground. Please tell me what you is your concern. I must get to my pupils."

Then, as if he did not know, he asked Tshering,

"Is Lamu with you, I did not see her on the playground this morning, is she ill?"

"The trouble is, Mr. Principal," stuttered Tshering, "Lamu will not be coming to school today, or any other day. She is getting married!" the Blow finally hit. Tshering looked at the Principal definantly.

Now it was time for Mr. Principal to hit back.

"Mr. Tshering, did you say, she is getting married, did she choose that? Or is she being forced by you, her own father, to do that? A girl who has done so well in school, she is liked and admired by her teachers, her contemporaries and her juniors. She is doing so well that we teachers were planning to send her records to

Loreto College in Darjeeling and request for an interview for her. She may even be awarded a scholarship. Do you know you will be destroying your child's life just because she is a daughter? How dare you?"

Mr. Tshering, who was fairly downcast now stood up, taller and broader than the slight scholarly Principal, banged on the desk and shouted,

"She is my daughter, and I will do with her what I like, how dare you question my authority?" and stamped out of the room.

The Principal shouted out to Tshering as he left, "Then it is on your conscience, you will ruin your daughter's life."

The Principal, put his head between his hand and suppressed a sob of despair, how many such ignorant, mean spirited fathers will he have to confront before it ends? How many more centuries and eons will it take to change men's attitude towards half of our race? But before he let Mr. Tshering leave the school premises scot free, he had to teach him a lesson. He rushed out of his office and rang a large brass bell which hung outside his class room for emergencies.

"Boing, boing, boing," the bell sounded

outside. In a matter of minutes, the play-ground, which was one of pandemonium, was in pin-drop silence – every pair of ears and eyes were trained on the Principal, who was now standing on a dais at one end of the play-ground,

He held a bull horn in his right hand, "Attention faculty, students and all members of the staff, I have a very important announcement." He looked at Mr. Tshering, who was desperately trying to sneak out of the school gates un-noticed.

"Ladies and Gentlemen, girls and boys, today, we have lost one of our best and favorite school mates, Lamu Tshering." Whispers and shaking heads were all abound on the play-ground, what did this mean? Lose, how lose? Is she sick, is she dying? Already some little ones were beginning to get teary and confused.

"Today, Mr. Tshering," here the Principal pointed the man who was trying to sneak out, "Lamu's father came to tell me that Lamu will not be coming to school anymore ." He paused and looked around the grounds. Heads were shaking with disbelief,

"NO, NO, NO!" came a universal roar from the children on the play- ground. Then, "Why, Why, Why?"

"He is marrying her to a total stranger, a man twice her age." All eyes turned to the creeeping Mr. Tshering, and the sound of "Boo" resounded across the school grounds.

One bold student shouted, "But why sir, she is my class-mate, I am the same age as her, and she always gets better marks than me, why are they forcing her to marry?"

Another student shouted, "she has only one more year, why not wait for only one more year?"

Then everyone started to add to the indignity, the confusion and total incomprehension. Mr. Tshering quietly slipped away in the confusion.

Back at home, Tshering vented his anger fully on his daughter. He grabbed her long hair and pulled her down to her knees. Mrs. Tshering and Nani rushed out to the verandah and tried to stop him.

"Husband, stop it, stop it. Lamu is your oldest and most beloved daughter, look at what you are doing!" shouted the mother.

"Arreh, betta," (oh, child) moaned Nani trying to put herself between her grand-daughter and son-in-law. "Please don't do this, she is a good girl, she will do as you say, but don't hurt her, you will anger the gods if you do."

Dolma and little Kancha came out to the verandah too and grabbed their father's leg and begged him to spare their oldest sister. Mr. Tshering suddenly let go of Lamu's hair and plonked down on the floor and wept.

"Oh, what have I done, I have given away my precious one, my hope, my joy." Then he wept and was inconsolable. Mrs. Tshering and Lamu held him in his arms.

"Husband, we do not have to give Lamu away,"

"Ayah wife, you do not understand, I have done a terrible thing. I am a gambler, all these years I have hidden my destroying habit from you because I knew it was evil, but I could not help it, it is like a demon who will not let go of me." He sobbed again.

"Ah, now I understand why we are not as well off as we should be, because our flower business is good, but somehow we never seem to have enough money even to buy our children new clothes for the New Year Festivities, or buy a new set of pots and pans instead of constantly repairing them, or a student-desk for Lamu, ahhhhh. May God forgive you."

"Or a new Bokku, (Tibetan gown) for you, my darling wife," chimed Mr. Tshering,

"Now I understand." Mrs. Tshering shook her head slowly and tears rolled down her cheeks which is just beginning to show signs of aging. "Oh husband, I wish you had told me, together we could have done something to get rid of your disease, for gambling is a disease."

"Now it is too late," groaned the man, "I have lost our daughter to one of the most hateful man in our village."

"What do you mean?" whispered his wife, not daring to mouth the words in case the demons act upon those words.

"It is a gambling debt I incurred two years back, I could not pay it, so Pemba said sweetly then,

"Oh, don't worry friend, you have something I have set my eye on for a long time, you can always give me that." Not knowing what he meant, Tshering agreed. "Cannot be anything that valuable, because I do not own anything valuable," Tshering had thought to himself. So, they made the agreement which, once made, cannot be rescinded. Now two years later, Pemba, threw the winning dice and turned to Tshering,

"Ah brother, you owe me quite a lot of money now, and I now want to collect;" he grinned. "Remember our agreement two years ago?"

"Yes," said Tshering, "You decided not to take payment until you were ready, "So what is it?"

Pemba's eyes grew large with greed and anticipation, "You will never guess what I want."

"Come on man," Tshering said, "I'm ready,"

"I do not think you are, remember, you cannot go back on our agreement, and these friends can be my witness of that night."

Tshering went through his mind and could not come up with anything he cannot part with.

"Your oldest daughter," whispered Pemba. The other players stopped and looked at the evil man, Tshering looked up at his old adversary, "Hahaha, you are joking, that is funny," he grinned nervously and fiddled with the dice. "You can't be serious, my daughter, Haha, she is only seventeen, and not yet finished High school."

Pemba eyes grew blacker and his face turned into an ugly disdainful scowl, his lips curled into a scornful smile, "Yes, I am serious, I have never been more serious in my life. I want my debt cleared, or...." He hesitated, "And it is of no use to say that you would kill yourself, because you do not have the guts to do that. I just want my debt cleared. I want your daughter."

Tshering could not believe what he had just

heard nor what he had done. The sky over him turned dark olive green and the wind was blown out of his body, he felt his spirit fly out through the top of his head and he dropped down on his knees like a man made of straw.

"Please brother, you cannot do that to me, she is the hope of our family, she the joy of my soul, she keeps us all sane and happy through all manner of illness and misfortune, please sacred brother, do not do this to us. I will give you my house, my thriving gladioli business, yes even my own life....." before he could finish, the other three friends chimed in also and pleaded for him.

"Bhaiya (brother) Pemba," they said, "do not do this, this is against Heaven, the gods will not be pleased. Tshering is offering you everything he has, taken it all, but don't take away his daughter." But Pemba only looked at them scornfully and shooed them away.

"Get out of my way, you pigs, do you think you are my friends, get out of my sight." They slinked away like so many defeated dogs with their tails between their legs. Meanwhile, Tshering, still on his knees, felt limp like a dirty dish rag thrown away, useless and unwanted.

His wife listened to his sad story with its tragic outcome.

"Papa," murmured Lamu, "Don't worry, I will marry him. I will do my best. I will wash and press his feet when he is tired, cook for him, wash and mend his clothes, keep his house neat and clean, grow vegetable in the garden, but I will NOT let him touch me." She buried her head under his arm pit and sobbed. "I will not let him touch me, unless he kills me." She emphasized.

"But daughter, that will never happen, he is a strong and powerful man, and he gets what he wants."

"Lamu," cried her mother, "My poor lovely Lamu, you are doomed, you will have a life of bitterness and suffering, and being a woman, you must bear it, and if you do have children, you must protect them from their own father," then she could go no further and burst into tears.

All this flashed through her mind's eye as everyone prepared her husband for the burial. Being Tibetans, it will be a "Sky Burial". First, they must prepare the body: it was broken at the knee and hip joints, and also at the elbow and wrist joints, so it could be made to sit in a full lotus position. Second, the body was dressed in the owner's best garments and placed in a small square palanquin. Lamu was slightly nervous when they came to dress him as she was afraid they might discover the weapon, which was still on him. Fortunately, they did not. As they carried the body up to the highest hilltop outside the town, everyone followed behind on foot. Lamu was flanked by her parents, while her siblings trailed in the back. As they trudged up the hill, the sky was already darkened by the arrival and swarming and winging of large well-fed vultures – the cleaners of our ravaged earth: ugly birds but necessary 'evils' protected by some cultures. At the top of the small table top hill there were three to four men waiting and ready with their knives, axes and other implements of death. It was not a comforting sight and almost made Lamu retch. Her father was the only family member who accompanied her, her mother stayed down below with her siblings. But looking around, she saw quite a gathering of strangers, this was odd she thought, who are they and why are they here, are they my husband's friends and unknown family members? She looked up at her father for reassurance,

"Alas," he answered her, "Even this very private affair of ours are now invaded by these tourists and voyeurs, they come to gape and stare and finally some of them even throw up. There is no respect anymore." He sighed.

The body was placed at a location pointed out by the four dead-body workers, who were armed and ready. The job will be done efficiently and quickly. Lamu took one more glance at her torturer and wished that his next reincarnation will not be too fearsome a creature. Quickly everyone left the scene, it was too much to bear even for the most curious of those tourists as they were herded away by their tour-guides.

Her mother accompanied Lamu to her little house. Lamu entered, heavy footed and heavy hearted though she thought she should have felt a burden lift off of her slender shoulders, instead, a kind of void preceded her into her the house, now hers.

"I cannot stay here, too many horrid and terrifying memories. I shall sell it, and with the money add another room to her parents' house and live with them. They are getting older now and can do with a little help around the house; I can get a teaching job at my old school and help with their finances." She thought. "Also, Tara will be in her last year in High School and may be going to college. She wants to be a nurse in the local hospital. She is a good girl, never gave me any trouble at all even when she was thirteen and all the other mothers were complaining about their daughters becoming uncooperative, disobedient and generally rude. Tara was not the cleverest girl in her class, but she was a hard worker and always passed her exams." Lamu was remembering her own school days, they were beautifully framed in the gallery of her past. She came out of her reverie and decided to sell the house as soon as possible. She and her mother cleaned and tidied up and threw away everything that belonged to her husband, there was nothing good enough to donate even to the poor. As she tossed them out, her feeling of cleansing and relief finally began to surface and a strange lightness filled her long-oppressed soul. She looked up and saw her mother staring at her,

"What is it Ma?" she asked, "Why are you staring at me like that?"

"Beta, it's just that I have not seen you smile for a very long time, it is good."

"Yes Ma, though I am now a widow, the feeling of relief and safeness is something I have never felt since that first night of our wedding, it is a wonderful feeling, seventeen years of being afraid, almost made me want to kill myself. It is the thought of Tara that kept me going and made me strong."

Her mother came over to her, took the broom from her hands and sat her down on the bed and took her in her arms like she used to do when she was little and was hurt or afraid.

"Oh, sweetie, how we have made you suffer. It is all our fault, we should never have let you marry that monster. Your and father and I committed a terrible crime against you and Heaven."

"Ma, it is over now, let us not talk about this ever again. I want to start life as if my star has just been born in the sky. I will sell this cursed house, take the money and build a new room in your house and come and live and take care of you and Pa and Nani for the rest of your lives." She smiled her once famous smile, took her mother's face in both her hands and kissed both her cheeks. "come Ma, let us get this cleaning done and get on with my new life."

That evening, after Lamu's mother had gone home, and Tara was with her friends, there was a soft knock on the door, "Now who can that be?" she thought, her original gut reaction was fear, trained by her drunken husband, then she realized that he would never cross that threshold again. She asked, "Who is that?" before opening it.

"It is Dr. Patel, I have come to see how you were doing."

She quickly opened the door, and greeted him with her customary smile, "Doctor, sahib. How nice to see you and how are you, come in, come in. Will you take some tea?"

"I am well," he said shyly, I was very worried about you, and came to see if I can help you in any way. You have had a terrible and terrifying life, and often I had wanted to come and see if I could be of any assistance, but never dared."

"Oh, doctor sahib, you are too kind, and yes, I too have often wanted to go to you to talk but was also kept away by fear. I wonder if there was anyone did not fear my husband, and whether he had any friends at all. Everyone seemed to keep out of his way all the time, even the 'pie-dogs'(feral dogs) used to cross the street when they saw him coming. It was so sad. I wonder what made him so angry all the time." She stopped for a moment, then added, "But let us not talk of him anymore, he is forever out of my life."

She went into the kitchen and brought out a tray of tea and a few samosas (fried spicy Indian vegetable dumplings) and started to pour him a cup of Darjeeling tea. She put the tea in front of him then looked at him earnestly and said quietly,

"Doctor sahib, I have something very important to say to you, and please don't interrupt me till I am done, then give me your honest advice as what I should do."

Dr. Patel had suspected that she had something to tell him. He had hoped that she would, which is why he came.

"Of course, I will to the best of my ability." He replied.

Then sitting primly on the small couch, she looked him in his eyes and began:

"My husband came home two Fridays nights ago, drunk and unbalanced as usual. He had wanted our daughter, Tara, to wash and press his feet, the demand terrified me, so I filled a basin of boiling water for Tara to take it to her father's feet. She gingerly took his feet and put them into the boiling water. He yelled, called her donkey, accused her wanting to kill him, and in his temper, he spilt the rest of the water on his legs, which immediately broke out into painful blisters. He screamed for me, I came to him with a towel over my left arm and hands, which was holding a heavy meat mallet. He tried to grab and pull me down, but being drunk and out of balance, he tripped and fell on the floor groaning with pain. I told Tara to run to her Grandma's house and not to say anything to anyone. Then I took the mallet and struck him on his head. He was winded. I knew I would not need to strike too hard because he would be inebriated and shaky. Then I dragged him on to the hated bed and arranged him comfortably on his back. He groaned with pleasure and did not wake up. Silently I went to his box of tools and nails, I found the hammer and a long thin three-inch nail I had been thinking about for a very long time and took it between my left thumb and index finger. I crept behind the bed and knelt behind my loathed husband, with hammer in my right hand, and nail in the left I aimed it at his foramen magnum, and with one swift blow it was embedded into his rotten brain. There was a silent sigh and the body went limp. I said a few "ohm mani padme hums," then arranged his thick black hair carefully around the nail-head, proceeded to tuck my now husband no-more into the quilt and made him look as comfortably asleep as was possible. There was no blood, no gore, no stain of any kind.

I then arranged the thin mattress on the floor beside the bed which was my sleeping 'quarters' after he had used me. I had thought I would not be able to sleep, but I slept so well, something I had not done for years, always wary that my husband would demand again!"

"The rest is public knowledge." She finished, breathed a sigh of relief, and looked away from Dr. Patel.

She was waiting for his verdict. He took her hands in his and made her look at him,

"Dear Lamu, the beautiful, long tortured and ever suffering brilliant woman," he looked at her for a very long time without another word.

"You have suffered and have been imprisoned longer than you deserve, I will not let you suffer another year, a day, a minute or even a second. This entire episode is swallowed up by those vultures – the Cleaners of the Mess we humans make."

Then Dr. Patel said, "Lamu, I did find the nail on that fateful night." A frightened look came across Lamu's soft round features,

"I think it is the most brilliant murder weapon and brilliantly placed, I have ever come across."

From before the beginning to after the end

Before I was born, I lived in a seemingly endless, lightless, airless and deliciously warm and wet world. I was lulled by a constant soft, even, lub- dub sound, interspersed with gently gurgling and sighing. I was want for nothing. Alas this did not last long, somehow, the space around me seemed to become smaller and smaller, or was it that I was growing larger, I don't know as I have no way of comparing myself to anything, except that I was beginning to feel rather cramped. I found it more and more difficult to move like I was used to, and kept bumping into the walls around me. Another strange phenomenon was that appendiges seemed to be growing out of me, and I began to imitate, autonomously, the lub-dub sounds which has been with me as long as I was in this place which, I was to learn later, is called womb. I also began to hear distant cooing's and melodious sounds which seem to be coming from outside of the womb–all very pleasing. Occasionally when I poked one appendage too far and hit the boundaries of my environment, I would hear happy sounds of surprise and adoration. Alas, life was no longer so comfortable anymore, I was feeling very crowded and pressed upon on all sides and began to thrash more and more, until I could no longer bear it and felt I must get out of this congested place, it was no longer a good place for me. I noticed ahead of me what seemed to be a small opening,

"Ah," I thought "if only I can push my way out of that, I may find more room to move about." Somehow, that part of me had grown enormously, and that was the part of me headed toward that tiny opening. How could I get the largest and heaviest part of me through that small hole and manage to go through it? So, I did most logical thing I could think of, I began to push. As I closed in on that opening, I began to hear the most terrifying noises coming from that hole. I tried to retreat. I was sure that was not the place I want to find room for myself, it was totally wrong. However, it seemed, I had no choice. Something seemed to be making me push in spite of myself, I was not aided by, which until then, was my quiet and comforting environment. It was trying to push me out with strong wave like movements pushing, pushing me towards that tiny hole. As

I neared it, that frightening noise became even louder and more terrifying, I stopped pushing, the shouting stopped, then another wave, anther push, more shouting, this backing and forthing seemed to go on forever. I was getting more and more fearful of going out of that hole. I was getting very tired, let me just lie quietly and go to sleep, I don't want to be pushed anymore, why can't I return to that nice lightless, airless, warm and wet place forever?

Then all of a sudden, there came a huge wave of contraction, the largest and heaviest part of me, popped through, there was no retreating now.

"Oooh, I see the head," shouted someone,

"So that's what they call it. Head." I said to myself.

I was coaxed out slowly by a pair of gentle hands, the shouting stopped, but, oh, the brightness of it all, even behind my closed eyes, but I was still awash in my warm liquid. Then something dreadful happened, I suddenly felt as if my lifeline had been cut, I no longer heard the constant comforting 'lub-dub' sound so familiar to me. I became suddenly alone and unconnected, only my own tiny lub-dub sound. What was happening, was this the end of me.

Then to add to all the injustices I experienced, in my vast, bright and noisy new environment, someone picked me up by my small appendages at the other of my head and hit me on my behind.

"Wah, wah, wah, wah," I yelled in reaction.

"Now that is a good healthy cry," said someone who sounded as if it was in charge, "You have a beautiful little baby girl, mother."

"So, I am a baby girl," I thought, whatever does that mean?" Then I was put onto my 'mother's belly, that was what I learnt later too, and someone covered us up, and spontaneously, my breathing synchronized with mother's. Both mother and infant fell into an exhausted and sound sleep. No one disturbed us. A long time later, my mother moaned, and discovered the other ladies had cleaned her up and disposed of her afterbirth. This was carefully wrapped in a clean piece of red brocade and stored away to be buried in a special place in the back garden. (In the twenty first century these afterbirths could well be used in stem-cell protocols). Mother looked down at me, still fast asleep on her belly. She smiled and said,

"Yes doctor, she is a beautiful baby." In my deep sleep, the other ladies, had cleaned me up and swaddled me in a lovely soft silken blanket and put me in the crook of my mother's arms.

We were surrounded by the entire family, my father, my grandmother, my mother's two younger sisters and two younger brothers. My grandfather was back from the front, fighting against the Japanese, because he was wounded in battle and had had a shrapnel, which had lodged in his right thigh, removed, and was sent home to recuperate. He looked at his first grand baby and sighed,

"I wish this baby girl will bring sunshine, peace and happiness everywhere. I will call her Pu-Chin." Alas I never did, human beings are still fighting each other everywhere, poor 'kung-kung,' (maternal grand- father in Chinese) never had his wish. I sincerely hope he is not mad at me.

HLASSA

My master was a poor rickshaw-walla (one who carries and pulls passengers in a rickshaw for a living), but in those days, there were not many customers, especially during the off-season times, because, after independence most of the English 'sahibs and memsahibs' had left to return to England. During the days of the British Raj, they used to come up from Calcutta to escape from the 'dreadful' heat and humidity of the plains to the cool mountain air of Darjeeling. So, my soon to be, master often whiled away the time gambling and drinking 'chhang' (an intoxicating brew made from fermented millet) with his fellow rickshaw pullers, or going to the market place to tease the women venders. One cold winter's day, he was sauntering around as usual, and wondered into the vegetable section, he used to like a particular vender there. He looked into a large basket of cabbages and found me hiding among the heads of cabbage and onions, trying to look like a head of cabbage, but I did not know that I was bigger than any of them and I was not green in color. He lifted me out of the basket and shouted,

"Hey Kanchi, what kind of cabbage is this, it must be bad, it has grown fur all over it." Kanchi, dressed in a Tibetan costume, came over; she was as short as she was wide with bright rosy cheeks and wide forehead.

"What did you say?" she demands her arms akimbo. She looked into the basket and saw me, "Areh!" she grabbed a short-handled broom and was about to strike,

"No no, wait a minute, wait a minute," said my master to be, "I didn't say I did not want the fury cabbage," I tried to bury myself deeper among the real cabbages, but he gently pulled me out, "I just said one of your cabbages is bad and has started to grow fur. I am going to take this little one and make a soup out of him, how much do you want for it?"

"Take it away, and go away," she scowled, "I don't know how he got in here. GO GO." By now I was trembling more from the thought of being a cabbage soup than from the cold. But my new master took me and tucked me into his smelly but warm boku (Tibetan garment), and before long I was contentedly asleep. Then I felt myself being pulled out from this wonderful haven and put into a large contraption on four wheels, and before me was a dish of rice and lentil curry. I was too hungry to complain, and within minutes all was gone. I was glad I was not still dependent on my mother's milk, but the thought of her suddenly made a strange and empty feeling come into my stomach, but almost as quickly, I forgot about her and wagged my little tail at my new master. "Oho, this is a clever little monster," he said, "come, I will call you Hlassa, because you are from my motherland, and I don't want to forget it. This is both my home, my bed and my livelihood," he said pointing to his large rickshaw, which can seat 4 adults face to face comfortably. But now you will share my home and bed with me."

Before long, I got used to his long, matted hair, which he tied back into a ponytail, and his loud but friendly voice. I am glad he did not bathe much, if at all, for I grew to love the smell of chhang and yak butter and cheese emanating from him. One day, my master was called to a job to carry a family up from the airline office. This family had just arrived from Calcutta and intended to settle in Darjeeling. There was an elderly lady with tiny feet who had a great deal of difficulty to walk up the slope of our town, so my master had to carry her to the rickshaw. There was an ahya (nurse maid) who was carrying a baby, and a little girl who squealed with delight when she saw me, she patted me on the head and wanted to hold me, because I was a 'loveable ball of fur by then-my master had fed me well. "Don't touch him," she was told, "he may have fleas." I was mortified, I did not even know what fleas were, though I did, as did my master also, itched a lot-something seemed to be biting us all the time. The other two members of the family were a tall handsome man who seemed very gentle and who was speaking softly to my master in his own language. The final person of the family was a very pretty lady with dark hair who seemed to be in charge, and she was the one who told the little girl I had fleas.

These must have been the father and mother of the little girl and baby. My master's rickshaw was rather large and heavily constructed with solid mahogany and brass fittings, and which can easily seat four grown adults. However, it needed four men, one at each corner, to carry and push it. All the while, I was in my master's boku with only my head sticking out. The ride was a short one to the family's home. The little girl desperately wanted to hold me, but was not permitted to do so. We often saw this family during their evening walks on Chowrastha and The Mall-a kind of promenade where one walked in the evenings, 'took in the air,' and met one's friends or simply had evening coffees in one of the 2 confectionaries. This was indeed a remnant of the British Raj. Whenever we met, the little girl would always come over to pet me, while her father would exchange a kind word or two with my Master in Tibetan. Later, I learnt that my master was a Khamba, a warrior tribe who roamed the mountains in Western Tibet near Khanding. They had been and were still valiantly fighting against the Chinese invaders. This also happened to be where the kindly gentleman had lived during his very early years. I grew to know this little family quite well. The Chowrastha-Mall walk was circular and about two miles around. On the opposite side of the circle one could see the full glory of the Mt. Kanchingjunga range-perpetually snow-covered, and rising to over 28,000', the third highest mountain in the world. All the inhabitants in this region were especially possessive of this range of mountains, and we considered that it belonged exclusively to us. Tourists would throng up to Darjeeling in May and again in October, just to get a glimpse of her, but she was often shrouded in gossamer mist or hidden behind clouds. The visitors would be lucky to see her once during their two-week holidays. One day, when I must have been about 6 months old in human terms, my master was especially kind to me, but he did something to me that was never done before, and which I detested. In fact, he tricked me into it. I was shown a large basin into which he put my favorite food. I thought it was a funny game-I was to eat my food in this strange hollow, perhaps he did not want me to run away before I had finished my meal because the sides were too high and slippery for a 6-month old puppy to climb out. He put me in and took me out several times, but the last time was quite different, as he picked me up and started to lower me gently into, hey the bowl was filled with rain, only this rain was quite warm and came up to my ears. I did not like it at all and started to yelp and whine and bark and tried to wriggle out of my master's hold. As I struggled, the warm rain got into my eyes and nose and worst of all into my ears. My eyes stung as if bitten by bees, my ears had sounds of the gurgling river, I could not breath through my nose, I was terrified, then to add insult to injury, my master started to rub something all over me, which welled into soft bubbles, and when I tried to lick it all off the taste also stung my tongue. I hated this white foamy stuff. After several minutes, my master poured away the rain, and I was rubbed dry with a familiar smelling cloth and then he tied me with a rope to dry in the sun. All the while he was telling me that I was to go and live with someone else-the lovely little girl who loved me so much. She was going to be 5 and I was to be her birthday present I would have a nice warm bed all my own, and live in the same house as that little girl. I would have the best food in town because the little girl's parent owned the best Chinese restaurant in Darjeeling. All the fleas on my body would be banished so I will not have to itch so much, and in any case my master said, "I will not be far away, and you can come and visit me any time you want." I did not understand a word, but I could see that my master had tears in his tough Khamba eyes. I cocked my head and tried to look intelligent and understanding, and I promised that I would be a brave and clever dog and do whatever he was telling me I should do. That afternoon my master took me to the restaurant, owned by the little girl's parents, and where there was a birthday party for her. There were several other little girls laughing and screaming at their games. I was excited by all the commotion, and wanted to join in the fun, but I was hidden in my master's boku. The pretty lady with the black hair then said to the little girl. "Come here darling, Papa and I have a surprise present for you." She came over, surprised to see my master. Then her father said to my master in Tibetan, "All right, you can take Hlassa out now." He pulled me out of his boku and handed me over to the little girl. She looked at her parents and her eyes grew bigger and bigger, then she screamed, clapped her hands and jumped up and down until her grandmother said, "Aya, foonla, foonla, foonla," (which means Oh dear, she has gone mad, mad, mad. The little girl grabbed me and held me so tightly that I thought I was going to lose all my breath-after all I was still only a puppy. I was immediately given a huge piece of cake on a plate; I gobbled up the cake and sat on the plat! Hoping for more. Then I was given sausages, noodles–Chinese eat 'long-life' noodles for their birthdays, so they have to be very long. I had lots of difficulty eating those long thin noodles and ended up getting horribly entangled. All the little girls laughed and clapped their hands as they saw what a mess I had become. I was in seventh heaven so that l did not even notice that my old master had quietly slipped away. All the little girls wanted to love me and hold me. I was the absolute center of attention of everyone, even more than the birthday girl. It was one of the happiest days of my life. That night I slept at the foot her bed, and it was to be my 'spot' for as long as could be. She was mine as much as I was hers.

As the October Puja (Autumn religious festival) holidays were approaching, my little mistress told me that her Jieh-jieh (older sister) was coming home for the holidays, and that she will be surprised to find a puppy at home. I was very curious about this Jieh-jieh: who was she, and was she a member of 'my' family, and if so, why was she living somewhere else, and had to 'come home' for the holidays? Was she kind, and would she love me as my little mistress did? The old lady with the small feet, my little mistress's grandmother whom she called "Po-Po" was saying to the servants, "Balla (she could not pronounce the word 'Burrah') Baby is coming home, get her room ready." Then one day, my little mistress, whom the servants called "Chhota Baby"-meaning 'small baby' as opposed to 'burrah', meaning 'big'-ran out of the house, "Jieh-jieh is home, lalala," she yelled with delight, she liked to yell and scream whether in anger or happiness, "Jie-jieh is home, Jieh-jieh is home." Up the street came a skinny person dressed in a navy-blue skirt and blazer, swinging a small attaché case in her right hand. On her head was a mass of black curly fur- almost as much fur as I had all over my body. My little mistress, her arms wide open, ran as fast as she could to meet her

Jieh-jieh. They collided in a shout of laughter and glee as the tall skinny one dropped her case and lifted my little mistress up into her arms. "Oh, Oh," she shouted in excitement. "Just see what I got for my birthday, you will love him, he is the most adorable thing in the world." My mistress squealed bursting with happiness. She wriggled out of her older sister's arms and ran towards the house. Of course, I was already out of the door and was sitting in the middle of the street, as I could not keep up with the speed my mistress's feet with my tiny ones, even though I had four. "You see, you see, isn't he adorable?" clapped my mistress. Her Jieh-jieh came up to me and bent down with a big grin on her face, she looked just like my mistress's daddy. She picked me up gently and cradled me on her shoulders and murmured, "Ooooooh he is so soft, cuddly and SO loveable," then turning to Chhota Baby, "What is his name?'

"Hlassa, but I call him Lassie. I know he is not at like the Lassie of the pictures, but I know he is just as clever, and if he ever gets lost, he will also come home just like that movie Lassie did."

"Where did you find him?"

"Mummy and Papa got him from Tenzing, the rickshaw man, for my birthday." "He is beautiful, and you will take good care of him, and not let Bobby pull his ears?" she laughed.

"Of course I will, and if Bobby pulls Lassie's ears, I will pull his too! Lassie sleeps at the foot of my bed and he loves mutton curry and rice, and he even drinks tea with milk and sugar." So once more I stole the limelight! One of the first things we did when Jieh-jieh came home was to go for a picnic at the Senchal Lakes. The cook prepared all sorts of goodies for us to take-cold five spice tea flavored eggs, chicken wings, different kinds of odd looking Chinese finger foods, some English sandwiches, and an assortment of pickled vegetables which the grown-ups seem to enjoy, but I could not stand them, and of course, piles of fruits. The servants packed blankets for everyone to sit on the grass, and a small stool for Po-Po to sit, who found it very difficult to get up after sitting upon the ground. I remember the first time Po-Po sat down, she almost did a back summersault, and when it came time to get up, three servants had to help her-one on each side to pull her and a third behind her to push her up-it was too funny for words, made even funnier for my little mistress and Jieh-jieh, when Popo got mad she clenched her false teeth with a loud clucking sound. We did not forget to take numerous umbrellas in case it rained, for Darjeeling, situated on the Eastern foothills of the Himalayas, is known for its torrential downpours during the monsoon season. Some-how we crammed everything into the trunk of the Hillman, and the rest of us into the car. I hated going in the car, though I liked to arrive, because, like my little mistress, we always got sick, and the car had to stop several times so that she and I could get out and vomit. Jieh-jieh tried to help by singing all sorts of songs to distract her, but of course I would not be distracted, and invariably got sick thus inducing my little mistress to also get sick. Then we had to stop the car and piled out for us to do the 'needful.' Back in again, this time with my head as far out of the car window as possible. My mistress sat in the front on Papa's lap. Mummy always liked to drive, which was very unusual because, 1) most people had drivers, and though we had one, she preferred to drive herself and 2) almost no women I ever saw, in those days, sat in the drivers' seat. Usually we took two cars, because some friends always accompanied us.

The Senchal Lakes, made up of two bodies of water, was the water supply for the entire town of about 25,000 people, and they were enormous. These for a small Tibetan terrier were terrifying and formidable. The sides were very steeply sloped, and I was afraid that one little mistake would make me slide into it, so I kept well away from the edge. Jieh-jieh was very excited for she loved to explore and immediately ran around one of the lakes-she disappeared from sight and we had to wait and wait for her to return before we were allowed to eat our scrumptious feast. She seemed to have gone for ages, and I was starving. The servants had already spread the blankets

and food baskets on the grass, and Bob-beh was toddling about, followed very closely by his Ahya. Popo was never comfortable at picnics and grumbled that we had perfectly elegant tables and chairs at home, there was fireplace to keep us dry and warm, and why did we have to come to this wilderness, spread our food on the ground and eat off of it like beggars and tramps! To cap it all, she detested the immediate collections of urchins and 'pie dogs' [ferrel dogs) who seem to materialize out of nowhere to stare at us. I especially did not like those mangy homeless creatures sniffing at us and at our food. I would have rushed at them had I been a bit bigger! After eating, it was required that everyone, including me, except for Po-Po, Bob-beh and Ahya to walk around the lakes. I loved this part of it, for I was so strong now and could walk for miles, I never seem to feel tired, perhaps it's because of my ancestors lived in the high Himalayas and herded their master's sheep and yaks. Near dusk, we packed up everything and headed for home, tired but happy and content. I slept in my mistress's lap most of the way-too tired to even to be sick and though Po-Po complained a lot, I think she secretly enjoyed herself too. Who would not? It was so peaceful and beautiful and we had all this all to ourselves. As long as we had those heavy monsoons, which lasts for three solid months a year, and those tall pine trees, which keep the soil from slipping down the mountain sides, the lakes will remain full and we will continue to picnic there. (Alas this was not to be so. Years later, one of them cracked and the local government never bothered to repair it. Over several years all the water leaked out and the lake dried. Furthermore, without control and supervision, many of the tall strong trees in the pine forest up the hillsides, which were holding the soil, were cut down for building, fire-wood, for whatever, this resulted in massive landslides during the Monsoons, which led to further damage of the lakes. Third, these

Lakes were made to provide water for 25,000 people, now there are 250,000 and more! Alas what future does Senchal has? (In fact, many, many years later, Jiej-lieh revisited her home town, and spontaneously burst into tears when she saw those terrible scars that gouged down the mountain sides-like so many battle wounds on a human body).

While Jiej-jieh was at home we went on many walks, as she liked to hike, explore and ride horses, but I thought my little mistress was a much better rider than her older sister. Almost every day we walked around the Mall, which was about 2 miles; in the early days, when I was still a puppy, my legs were short and my body so fat and round that my belly almost touched the ground, those were the longest two miles I had ever known. Almost always, less than half the way around, I would sit down and cry to be carried. My family thought that was very funny, but it was not at all to me, my little mistress would try to push me gently from behind and I would try to go a few more steps only to sit down again with exhaustion, or they would continue to walk on ahead pretending leave me behind, then I would yelp and whine, finally, after many pitiful cries, Jieh-jieh would pick me up and carry me the rest of the way. Or sometimes, they would put me into the stroller with Bob-beh, which neither of us liked. I think there is a photograph of us together in the stroller, both with unhappy frowns on our foreheads. However, when I got older and stronger and I was not so fat and round anymore, I even used to run after the horses JiehJIeh and Chhota-Baby rode.

In fact, I was the bane of all the riders who rode up or down our street. I particularly hated those horses who cantered, I would run out of the house and bark and try to nip their hoofs, not knowing that if I got hit once, I would be dead! Humans called this "ignorance is bliss," and 'tis folly to be wise," but I never understood what it meant. Though I was only two feet high and weighed less than twenty pounds, I had the heart of a lion, and often fancied myself as the "king of the road." I strutted up and down our street, challenged any dog that came along, charged at any horse who dared to go faster than a walk, and terrified those mangy ugly beasts humans call 'cats.' One day, I was sitting in my usual place on our verandah, which overlooked the street, surveying everything that walked down below, I saw a strange tall black creature come bounding down, at the same time, my little mistress came running to her mother shouting, "Mummy mummy, I saw a sheep that looks like......... a dog," she hesitated, "no, no I saw a dog that looks......... like a sheep...... I......" she stopped in confusion. Jieh- jieh looked over the verandah and laughed, "Ah, it is a standard size poodle, yes it does look like a sheep, see, and even Lassie is confused." I heard my name and cocked my head and ears this way and that in agreement. I did not want to challenge this creature. Whenever we went on one of our walks and passed Tenzing's rickshaw stand, I would run to my old master, running and wagging my tail all the while so people thought I would wag off my entire rear-end altogether."

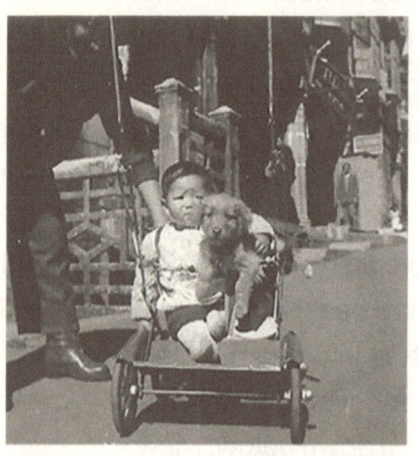

"Ah Hlassa, you have not forgotten your old master, you are indeed handsome now, your fur shines like gold. Your new-owners must love you very much." I simply wagged my tail some more and ran back to my little mistress. Sometimes, I was naughty and would "run-away" and spend a night with my old master, the next day, Tempa, our servant would always fine me there.

Life was blissful in those days. But then came a time when my mistress had to go to the same place as her Jieh-jeih, where there were many girls all dressed in the same navy-blue skirts and while blouses. It was called a boarding school, and they went to learn all sorts of things. The bigger people, called nuns, wore long black robes, which covered everything except their faces and hands. As they walked the robes wished about at their feet, and around their waist they hung long strands of large beads with a large wooden thing, with a long and a short arm at the end. I kept my distance from them, because if this struck you, it would surely hurt. I missed my little mistress a great deal and waited impatiently for her to come home, but I did become accustomed to her absence and waited for her return during the week-ends and holidays.

One day, I was lying sleepily in the sun on our verandah, when I suddenly heard a distant voice calling breathlessly, "Come back, Yin-Chin, come back to school, I will not punish you if you do," over and over again. I at once took a great interest and looked out onto the street, and there was my mistress with a huge grin on her face, and I ran to I meet her. She had decided that she did not want to stay in school and so ran out of the gates. One of nuns saw her and began to chase her. Her chain of rosary beads clattering about her waist, her face brilliantly red, arrived at our house, and breathlessly said to my mistress's mother,

"Jesus, Mary and Joseph, she just decided to run away," pant, pant, "Oh dear, what will mother Superior say?" She was quite distraught. Meanwhile, my little mistress had a satisfied grin on her face, and I was very proud of her, but her mummy was not very pleased.

"Darling, why did you do that? See how exhausted poor Sister Lucinda is, you have made her run so hard, and all the way up the hill."

"I don't know, I just wanted to see Lassie, and I wanted to come home, I don't like school, and I'm scared of those nuns."

"Oh Darling, we know you love Lassie, but that

does not mean you must run away from school to her. You are in the best school in India, and you must stay there and learn." In the background, I could see my mistress's Papa quietly suppressing a smile, he too was proud of his little seven-year old daughter who could out run a grown woman, and all the way up that hill at that.

"I am terribly sorry Sister Lucinda, we will take you and our daughter back to school in our car, and I am sure this will not happen again."

One year, during the girls' Winter holidays, when I was about 4 years old, and my mistress about 9, we were all woken up before the sun was even awake. There was a hush in the air, but everyone was very busy with lots of bags and suitcases. I stayed curled in my basket in the kitchen, (I had been relegated to the kitchen as I got older and my mistress had gone to school) and watched as everyone busied themselves with this and that. Jieh-jieh eyes were red as were my mistress's, and grandma was rocking herself back and forth, mumbling something about Jieh-jieh going away to a land very far away from Darjeeling and that we would probably never never see her again. Tenzing, my old master, the rickshaw puller and his helpers were outside waiting. When everything was packed into it, grandma stayed at home with Bob-beh, my mistress's little brother, and who was about the same age as me, and Ayah, the maid. Then Jieh-jieh came over to my basket and patted me on the head, ruffed my fur all over my body so it made me feel all warm, but oddly sad, because I sensed that I would indeed never see her again. "Be good, Lassie, bye-bye." Then she walked out of the door. I suddenly yelped and leaped out of my basket and ran to catch up with the rickshaw. I ran as fast as I could, because by then I was a pretty fast little golden Tibetan terrier. It was quite scary because the street was very quiet as all the shops were closed and there was nobody about. I caught up to them at the travel office just in time to see Jieh-jieh and 'Mummy" climb into the taxi to take them to the big rickshaw that flew like birds. I dashed to the car, wagging my tail as hard as I could; Jieh-jieh gave me one final rub on the head and was gone. I crept to my mistress who was sobbing her heart out in her "papa's" arms. He looked proud but sad, also with the same question in his eyes: "Will I ever see my oldest daughter again?" Where was Jieh-jieh going that she might never be seen again? Why was she going so far anyway? All I heard was something about becoming a doctor in a land called America. This was the first of many partings, which seemed to sadden everyone, yet it was tempered with a kind of gladness and pride. Certainly, when my family was asked about the whereabouts of Pu-Chin, they answered with some pride, "She has gone to university in America." I wondered about this but not for long, I ran to my little mistress, tried to jump up to her and get her to catch me. Soon all was forgotten and we ran home. The house seemed unusually quiet and for some time, and during the holidays, only my mistress came home, and I forgot about the tall skinny girl with the mop of black curly fur on her head, and who looked so much like my little mistress's Papa, and simply concentrated on becoming and being the "king of the road." After a very long time, my mistress's Mummy came home, but without Jieh-jieh.

There was a lot of tension in the air and I often heard my mistress's parents whisper late into the nights. Even Po-po (my mistress's grandmother) looked worried and began chant 'o mi to fu' with her prayer beads more and more. One day, Mummy brought my mistress home from school, even though it was not a holiday, and I heard her telling my mistress,

"Darling Mummy must also go away for a very long trip, but I will come home now and then to visit all of you, and perhaps, one day, you will all join me in my new place." My mistress begged her not to let her be a boarder in school any more, saying "I am older now and I could help look after Po-po and Bob-beh at home, and help Papa in the restaurant. Since Jieh-jieh is gone, I could have her room instead of sharing a room with Popo and Bob-beh." Mummy consulted with Papa and finally it was decided that she would no longer live in school but become a day-scholar, i.e. go to school every day but live at home. My little mistress was delighted and, as usual, jumped up and down for joy. Then, on that fateful morning, like before, the house was full of bags and baggage, Tenzing was, once more, waiting outside to take us to the travel office. There was the same hushed air about, but Popo was the most distressed of all, she simply could not be consoled, she could not stop crying and wailing and was convinced that she would never see her daughter again, and she was right, for indeed, she never again saw her favorite daughter, who never did return to Darjeeling. At first, I started to run after the taxi, and barked and barked, for I too felt that this was not good, and that my mistress's own mummy was going away forever. I too loved her very much and did not want to see her go.

This was the second parting, and the feeling I had for it was not good. This time there was neither joy nor pride associated with it, and Po-po was inconsolable for days after and never did recover from her loss. Papa was extremely quiet and had an air of despondency about him, but he had two children, a mother-in-law to take care of, and a restaurant to run, so he had to carry on.

Of all the people I knew, Po-po was the saddest of them all, even though, she could be very funny sometimes. She loved to laugh and giggle with my mistress and Jieh-jieh. She used to have a daily conversation with a certain Colonel Mercer every morning as they crossed paths during their morning constitutional-he on the way to the Gym-Khana Club, and she on the way to the restaurant-neither spoke the other's language. I used to sit on the road and wait until they finished their conversation. Of course, I understood them both. "Pani lai la," Popo would begin, meaning it's going to rain, 'pani' is Hindi for water, and 'lai la' means 'coming' in Chinese.

"Yes, yes, I'm going to the Gym-Khana Club."
"Chir le fan ma?" (Have you eaten?)

"Wednesdays, they have a special tennis match in the Gym-Khana." Thus they would go on for a few minutes.

Then Colonel lifted his hat and said, "Goodbye." Popo too would wave her hand and say, "bye bye."

But when my mistress told Popo that she was moving out of their shared room to take over Jieh-jieh's room, she was distraught. She wrung her hands and cried, "Ahya, you are leaving me too, I didn't mean to be angry with you the other day, so what if you spilled the milk all over the floor, please, do not leave our room," and she started to cry.

"You will have Bob-beh with you in the room still, there will be more space for both of you. In any case Jieh-Jieh's room has no one in it, and it is a waste." I consoled her and started to move my things anyway.

People in town were talking in soft voices, and Papa spent a lot of time talking to Tenzing, the rickshaw puller. I knew they spoke about horses-who had them, where they were supposed to be sent and pick up someone very important. All this had to be done in absolute secrecy. This went on for several weeks, then suddenly one day, there was much rejoicing in town, everyone had big smiles on their faces, particularly my old master and his Tibetan friends. It must be that the important man had arrived. There was a very festive air all over the town and the Tibetan ladies came out in their very colorful brocade 'bokus'- long Tibetan dresses, and the men in their one-armed garments, swash buckling belts and their tall embroidered wool boots. One day a large man with a big nose and a red face, who had a mop of reddish fur not only on top of his head, but also at the bottom of his chin, boomed into our restaurant and demanded to use the phone. He wanted to send a telegram to London to announce to the world of the news that His Holiness, the Dalai Lama had successfully escaped from Tibet and therefore the clutches of the Chinese Government. Everyone was astonished as we heard him dictate his message over the phone. We were also amazed that he could actually send a message through the telephone from the remote little hill station, Darjeeling, in the North-East corner of the Himalayas half way across the world to famous London, England. Everyone was speechless and awe struck when Mr. George Patterson, the large bearded man announced, "Now the world knows it! This is a grand day. His Holiness has successfully escaped from the tyranny of Mao Zhe Dong." But to my little dog-brain, I thought it was also sad that this young King had to leave his own country and his own people in order to survive. During those few days, my mistress' father visited the young King's family often, but I was never allowed to go with them because they had many fierce lassa-apsos-little yappy, bad tempered dogs whose hair covered their eyes and whose lower jaws jutted out beyond the upper ones. I often wondered how those poor cousins of mine were able to see or eat anything. No wonder they had such bad tempers! But I was jealous that Bob-beh was allowed to go, because he used to play with this young King's youngest nephew. I had always considered myself above Bob-beh in our family hierarchy.

One day, a few days after His arrival, people started to gather in Chowrastha-a kind of plaza where one could sit and gossip, eat some snacks or simply look at our mountains, those part of the Himalayas the people always considered 'our' own. There used to be a saying, "if you want to meet someone, just go to Chowrastha and you will be sure to meet that person sooner or later." Suddenly, there was a hush and whispers passed along the crowd, "He is here, He is here, oh, how young He is." Who is here I wondered, a passage parted leading up to an erstwhile podium which had been set up at one end of the plaza, then a young man, not much older than Jieh-jieh, walked, straight backed and slowly, looking and bowing to his left and right as he approached the dais. He got up on the platform, looked around and greeted everyone palm to palm, and eyes twinkling, smiled and giggled. His now famous giggle. He told us about his great and difficult journey through and across the Himalayas to escape from the Chinese,

"I have slipped out of Tibet away from the Chinese," here He smiled at everyone and giggled again, He was able to joke even at a time like that. "Perhaps one day, I will be able to return to my people." There was no blame, no incriminations, no anger; it was just a simple statement of fact. "I have slipped ...." Then He remonstrated that people nowadays had forgotten how to say the mantra (holy chant) "Ohm mani padme hum." So, He started to teach the assembled crowd how to say it correctly, and when everyone said it in unison, the whole town reverberated as if trying to waken the gods to witness the goodness of this young monk, even I, a dog, understood what was going on. The sense of jubilation was in everyone's soul during those few days that he was with us in Darjeeling. But one day, there was no sign of Him, just as he had "slipped away from the Chinese," so He had slipped away from us. The Indian

Government, under Prime Minister, Jawaharlal Nehru, had prepared a new abode for Him on the other end of the Himalayan chain, Dharamsala, where he and his exiled Tibetan Government still reside.

One winter, Mummy asked my mistress and Bob-beh to join her in Kathmandu, which was where she had gone, and to take Ahya and me along. We were to go there for our winter holidays. It was a trip I would never forget. We did not go by the rickshaw that could fly, but one that was extremely long like a monster snake with a huge blackhead that belched enormous black clouds of smoke, and now and then gave off ear-splitting screams. I was terrified. But when my young mistress read a sign that said 'NO DOGS ALLOWED ON THE TRAIN' she was even more terrified, she did not want me to be separated from my family. She took me up into the upper bunk with her and covered me with her thick quilt and told me to keep really quiet, luckily, I understood human language by then. The guard came through the train, for this was what they called this long smoke-belching snake like rickshaw, checking each compartment, and I was sure my shivering body would give me away, or the soft quilt would make me sneeze, but we managed to deceive the guard and the train pulled away from the station leaving behind a mass of people of all sorts of shapes, sizes and smells, all wrapped up in their various types of garments and head gear, and surrounded by masses of boxes, luggage, bags and bundles. It was the longest trip I can remember. Leaving the coolness of Darjeeling was a nightmare in itself for I had never experienced such heat, dust, and unknown smells most of which was not pleasant, and the level of noise- people shouting, bells ringing, trains puffing, car horns honking, things clanging, banging-was deafening almost beyond the tolerance of a little dog's ears. Luckily, I was not at all inclined to eat, so I kept out of sight for most of the journey. After what seemed like days, weeks, years, centuries, aye an eternity, the air began to feel familiarly cool again. I slowly peeked out of the quilt, I could see hills, things I was used to and loved. The noise had also died down and my mistress and Bob-beh and Ayha seem animated. "We are nearly there,' said my mistress, "We will soon be with Mummy, Hoorah." If we had room, I am sure she would have jumped up and down, as she liked to do when she was happy. Our short and round Ayha was relieved that we had arrived safely.

'Mummy' was at the station waiting for us. She

was overjoyed to see us, but my mistress and Bob-beh and I were too overwhelmed and tired to say anything. We all missed our Darjeeling and the things familiar, and though we were happy to see Mummy, we were stunned. She had started a small inn and restaurant just outside town, and had a beauty salon where ladies came to have their hair washed and curled-a thing a little dog like me never understood-all that trouble, all that strange 'rain', all that stinky liquid just to make their 'fur' curly. Many people came to the inn to eat and drink and it was considered to be the most fashionable place to "be seen." There was a small garden with soft green grass, which was surrounded by flowering shrubs and other sweet smelling bushes. I used to love to lie on the grass in the sun. We stayed in Kathmandu through the holidays, but I do not remember much what we did because there were so many new things and people to keep my eyes on, particularly so many 'pi dogs' to ward off. 'Pi' dogs were not really wild, but dogs who have no home, or whose foreign masters, when they went back to their own countries, had left them behind, so most of them were very angry and nasty because they were abandoned- unloved, unfed and unkempt, I suppose in a way, they were like homeless people.

But I had no sympathy for them; in fact, I was rather scornful of them and hated them. It was an arrogance I was to pay for dearly. My mistress and Bob-beh had to return to Darjeeling to resume school, but Mummy decided to keep Ahya to help her in the salon, and me, in Kathmandu with her. I was very sad, and desperately missed my mistress and 'Bob-beh-' for they used to take me everywhere with them on their numerous escapades. Left to my own devises, I once again resumed my role as the "King of the road," only this time there were too many contenders- some far bigger and rougher, gangster-types, than me, so I used to get into awful fights, though I was a small dog, I never lost my attitude of a big one. Many, many times Mummy had to save me, and the servants had to drive those 'pi dogs' away with large sticks and stones. But it was of no use, they hated and envied my good life and would attack me, unprovoked, at the least little opportunity. One day, they almost killed me, Mummy found me outside our gate, my ears were torn off eyes almost blinded and gaping flesh where they had viciously bitten me. She carried me to her room, bathed me gently and covered my wounds with a soothing salve. Mummy used to be an army nurse during the Second World War in the front lines, so she was used to this kind of injury. She wrapped me up in a soft blanket and sat with me night and day, feeding me chicken soup, at first with an eyedropper, and later as I improved, with a spoon. Gradually I returned from death. It was a miracle, and I was able to eat soft foods by myself. It was then that Mummy decided to send me back to Darjeeling to be with my mistress, Bob-beh, Popo and Papa. Though I had missed my mistress terribly, those three months of nursing that Mummy gave me, made my soul tied to her forever. So once again I had to travel back on that dreaded long, smoke belching, black-fire-headed, loud rickshaw, only this time it was with Tempa-one of Mummy's most trusted servants. One can imagine the joy and screams and jumping's of up and down my mistress did when we were reunited. Bob- beh, being older now, thought all that exhibitionism was not cool. But he too could not contain his own joy for long, for I saw him shed a secret little tear when he took me into his arms. Of course, Popo and Papa were also delighted. My mistress had grown up a lot in those few months. She helped Papa in the restaurant in the evenings and during the weekends, and saw to it that Bob-beh attended school and did his homework. I used to accompany him to school every morning, and sometimes I raced him to it. But I always stopped at the gate, and did not leave until I saw him go into the building. My mistress' school was much further away so I did not go with her, but I always knew when she would return and would wait for her in the middle of the road, because in those days, no cars were allowed on the street where we lived. The moment she saw me she would run the last stretch to meet me. But things were not good. People, who used to come to see Papa, came less often, and business at the restaurant went from bad to worse, as if people were afraid of us and were avoiding us. There was much talk of fighting and attacks in the India/ China borders areas. I did not understand at all what all this meant but, in my heart, I knew something was not right. I sensed and dreaded every day of some unknown doom. Came, it did. One Sunday afternoon, Papa was just teaching my mistress how to make French toast, when there was a loud rude knock on our door. I barked fiercely and growled at the door because I did not like the smell of the people on the other side. Bob-beh went to open it, four policemen demanded loudly to see my mistress's father. Papa went outside to talk to them, all we heard was a lot of muffled conversation, while Popo rung her hands and rocked in her chair as she did before. Like me, she did not understand a word either, but also, like me, she did not like those men and sensed foreboding doom. My mistress and Bob-beh waited patiently in the living room. After a while, Papa returned with a pale and stunned expression on his face, he turned to my mistress who was hardly fourteen years old then, "Darling, I have to take a short trip, take care of your grandma and little brother. Look after things for a while, I will try to be back soon." He turned to those men who took him away. He was never to see our flat again. I jumped into my mistress's lap and tried to offer what comfort I had. We sat silently in the semi darkness of the living room, our French toasts, dry and greasy in the frying pan were totally forgotten. Popo continued to rock and moan, she had been through this before in China during the Sino-Japanese war, only it was many times worse than this. My mistress told Bob-beh and Popo that Papa will return soon, so we had just to wait and continue our life as it was. But Papa did not come back, not for three days, not for a week, not for two, we were worried, but we continued to wait. Many days later, a friendly Chinese lady came to the house and stayed with us to help us out. We had no idea who she was or how she knew we needed help; we only knew that she was a friend. Finally, one day, after about two weeks, another knock came on our door, this time I was frantic with excitement and happiness, I created quite a wind with my tail wagging. Bob-beh ran to open the door and there stood Tenzing, tears running down his weathered face. Bob-beh pulled him into the flat and made him sit down on the sofa. Through his sobs, he told my little family that Papa had been taken to the prison. My mistress did not even know the word for prison in Chinese as she tried to explain to Popo what had happened and tried to describe to her that he was locked up. But there was no need, Popo had understood as soon as she saw Tenzing's face. He said that the food in the prison was horrible, that we should take something for him and he would show us how to get to the prison. So everyday, my mistress, Bob-beh accompanied by the nice Chinese lady and Tenzing, with me in tow, went to the prison to visit Papa. I stayed with Tenzing while they visited, as dogs were not allowed inside. But things did not improve. On another day, a Chinese friend of Papa's came and warned us that we may be visited by some other policemen, that we were to burn all papers and not let them find anything. He left as quickly as he came. His warning was true, meanwhile my mistress and Bob-beh burnt any papers they thought important in the fireplace, and none too soon, just as they were to burn the last bundle there came a very loud bang on the door, "Open up, this is the police!" My mistress thrust this last bundle under my blanket in my basket and told me to lie in there, not make a sound and no to move. She opened the door, the nasty men pushed past her into our flat. They rummaged everywhere, turning our cupboards, drawers, looking under sofas, tables, whatever they could lay their hands was turned upside down. We did not know for what they were searching, they even ransacked the kitchen, where I lay in my basket. One of the men bent down to search my basket, I gave a fierce growl and bared my teeth at him, then my mistress said in a cool voice, "be careful, he will bite, and he has some kind of disease!" The hand was quickly withdrawn. The papers were saved. The Indian Government began to round up all the Chinese in the border areas, whatever their political inclinations. In fact, Papa, a strong anti-communist and a Kuo Ming Tang supporter, at the time of his arrest, had been collecting thousands of rupees from the Chinese people in Darjeeling to donate to the local Indian government in support of their cause against the Chinese Communist. In my doggy-heart, I knew something was going to happen, Tenzing was coming more and more often to our flat and took me with him "to play". Then one day, they came. These men with the awful smell came to take my mistress, Bob-beh and Popo with her tiny bound feet, away. My mistress was very brave, she came to me in my basket, patted my head and said, "Lassie, be a good doggie." I never saw her again. My old master took me home to his rickshaw, though he had no business now, he still 'lived' in it – it was his home. I often used to go to our old flat on the third floor of the building, and sat outside our door, waiting and hoping to see my little mistress open it and call me inside. Or I would walk around the Mall thinking she may be taking her evening walk with Mummy and Papa and Bob-beh. I even went to the stables to visits the stable boys, but they would just pat my head and say, "Hlassa, Chhotta Baby is gone, she will not come back again." Sometimes I went to the restaurant to see if my mistress' Mummy would be there, and again sometimes, at night I would listen intently hoping to hear my mistress's Papa talking to my old master in Khamba. In those days, I still felt as if I were the "King of the road." But strange, I was beginning to feel tired, and chasing those horses no longer gave me the feeling of power, even the mangy cats did not irritate me anymore. I seem to be sleeping more and more and my temper was getting worse and worse, not that I was good tempered in the best of days, and people did not want to come near me anymore; and my golden hair had become dull and thin. I did not care, I preferred to sleep and 'see' my mistress and little Bob-beh run up the road, or share a birthday cake with them and get all tangled up in those long-life noodles, or chase around Chowrastha, or be hugged tightly by my mistress and smell her delicious sweet scent. Sometimes, the tall handsome man with the curly hair, or the black hair lady who had saved my life from those horrid mangy dogs, would flash in my sleep, and sometimes the person my mistress had called Jieh-jieh would smile down at me. One evening, I was all curled up in my old master's rickshaw, I heard a distant voice calling me, calling me, "Lassie, Lassie ... My little mistress had come to get me at last. I opened my eyes and looked up, my old master was all a blur, and he was shaking his head and then black. "Ah Hlassa, you old cabbage, tashe delek." Goodbye.

Hurricane Surfing

"Hurricane Hermione is gathering force and coming up the eastern shore. There is gale force wind and severe flooding in parts of Florida already. We recommend you stay at home and avoid any unnecessary travels," were the words that came over the radio over and over again, ad infinitum. The more they heard them, the more excited they became. The family and had planned to visit a friend in Virginia Beach over the Memorial Day week end and were rather excited to think that they may encounter a hurricane! The night before, a couple of concerned close friends had rung to say,

"Have you heard the radio?"

"yes, we have," the mother answered.

"So, you are not going to VB?"

"Yes, we are," she said

"Have you seen the TV weather channel?"

"No, I have not, but I will."

"You are not going, are you?"

She could visualize them shaking their heads and rolling their eyes at their madness, but nevertheless, was grateful for all these calls, she wished she could have been more comforting to her concerned and well-wishing friends............ They had decided to go, her son and his wife and their three beautiful daughters, and her daughter had no doubts at all that they would be going. Certainly, they will be very disappointed if they decided not to go. So, what is a little wind and rain?

On that steel-grey, cloud-capped morning, there was no need for any alarm clocks, because all the kids were already dressed, very excited and ready to go. They had even packed their individual backpacks and were neatly piled near the front door. Someone had even started breakfast: there was a pile of toasts gently drying and cooling in the toast rack, which is why the English toasts always came out hard and cold.

Noel, the brother-in-law cleverly named this very English and ubiquitous kitchen gadget "toast-drying and cooling-devise."

Another grand-child was shouting,

"Cereal, eggs, marmite or jam anyone? Tea is in the pot so you lot grown- ups please sit down at the dining table and eat, before the Hermione forces us to stay home!"

Dutifully the "grown-ups" sat down to breakfast, they looked at each other and thought in unison,

"Ah ha, we should do this more often, this is how we can get our breakfasts cooked for us!" They could not have eaten any faster as the kids urged everyone to hurry, and even before mother finished the last bite of her cold dry toast, her plate was snatched from her and taken to the sink. By the time everyone had finished, the dishes and cutlery were washed and put into the drying rack, and the young ones were hurrying out the door to load the car.

All the beach bags had been packed the night before and were ready to go. They loaded their van with mats, bogy-boards paddle boards, ratts, and other beach toys, and struggling against the quickening wind and rain, they headed for Interstate 95 in search of a hurricane.

Luckily, many people did heed the dreaded weather warning and stayed home, so the infamous 95 was rather "free" of traffic. As they travelled south and neared Virginia Beach, the clouds became angrier, as if challenging them to continue, the raindrops were wee marbles bouncing off the wind shield and the roads were strewn with more and more debris around which they had to weave and meander. The mother's brother, who lived in Florida and was used to, and loved such heavy weather, had warned them about flying debris, meaning man-made ones, fortunately there were none of those kinds on the freeway, the debris they encountered were mostly branches, tons of leaves and some larger tree limbs.

About two and a half hours into our journey, some shouted, "Anyone hungry?"

"You bet, we are!" was the answer in unison.

Sandwiches were passed around, and a flask of piping hot tea sweetened with condensed milk, another surprise the younger children had brought with them. They must have been up half the night getting ready for this road trip. They were the best peanut butter and jelly sandwiches they had ever eaten, no one even bothered to ask who had made them. They drove down the main boulevard of Virginia Beach solo. There were no cars anywhere. It was quite eerie like a science fiction film set, the monster could be hiding behind anyone of those high-rise condos.

They arrived at Anne's house in record time.

She was surprised but thrilled to see them when they rang the doorbell.

"Oh, I am so glad to see you all, I was afraid you would cancel," she joyfully exclaimed.

"Are you kidding?" Her friend asked, "My family quit because of a common or garden hurricane? No Never."

In fact, one of her own sons had phoned to ask whether the hurricane had arrived and were the waves large enough for bogy-boarding, body surf and real surfing. She had said that it was definitely too large and dangerous, and told him not to come.

When they stepped out of the car, there was a distinctive smell, or more like a presence in the air, kind of electrical, almost spicy sort of taste to it, simultaneously we all opened our mouths and took a bite......" Ha-ha," laughed their friend, "Yes eat all the ozone you like, its free and 'on the house.'" They had never experienced this before, not unpleasant. The thought of 'biting and gobbling' ozone made them feel rather virtuous and fortunate.

The younger members of the group immediately headed for the beach. The mother followed slower as the wind had an easier time with a septuagenarian than the younger crowd. By the time they came to the beach, she had to stop, and grab hold of the steel railing on the edge of the ramp going down to the sands. The rest of the family battled valiantly against the assault of driving, bee-sting-like sand. However, in spite of shorts, tank-tops and hatless (just as well), they forged and ploughed on, their angle against the hurricane-force wind getting ever more acute, so that by the time they arrived at the water's edge, they were almost at 45 degrees to the ground, just to keep 'upright.' The 10-year-old youngest granddaughter had to grab on to her father's arm to keep from being blown away. As soon as they reached the water's edge, her grown daughter waded fearlessly out into the water up to her waist. She had just come from damp, misty and chilly England, she was determined to go to the beach and into some warm ocean waters, literally come gale or high water.

After this quick initiation, they struggled back to the friend's house, adrenalin coursing through their veins and their faces blown into permanent goulash grins.

"How was it? Was it frightening? How did the little one?" she exclaimed excitedly,

"It was fantastic," said the young ones, all shouting at once, "and we even got in the water,"

"What? No! you did not! Weren't the waves frighteningly rough and high?"

"Ya, but we did not mind, the red flag was out, and we were the only ones on the beach, but there were no life guards to tell us not to go in the water, and Aunty is a very good and strong swimmer, she ran straightaway into the waves, laughing her head off, she will not let any of us drown."

"It was absolutely wonderful, the little fear added that much more excitement." aunty said.

"But what about Nora," Anne asked anxiously, "She didn't go in did she?"

"Oh, she's too chicken," said an older sister, "She clung to Dad all the time, phu!"

"Of course, she had to, otherwise she would have been blown away," said another older sister.

"Blown away," said my friend, "You mean to say the wind was so strong that a ten-year old girl could have been blown away?" she asked, realizing that bad things could have happened. She sat down, put her head between her hands and groaned.

"Alright, I am glad you all are here, you all must be starved, I have made a large pot of beef stew and a loaf of garlic bread, and a big bowl of nice green salad. Go have a shower and come back as quickly as you all can."

Everyone rushed to the two bathrooms, and a couple to the outside shower, which had a mixture of hot water and refreshing rain.

When everyone was showered, clean and dry, and were sitting down at the dining table, with bowlfuls of hot beef stew in front of them, and spoons in hand ready to 'chow down," there was a loud banging on the front door!

"Oh dear," said Anne rather nervously "I wonder, who could that be."

"Mom, open the door, its cold out here." Someone outside shouted, she went to the door and was barely able to open it because of the wind, with her pushing and the person outside pulling, they managed to open the door. Standing outside was her totally crazy son, a tall, six-foot four-inch, skinny young man with windblown shoulder length hair and a wild animated look about his eyes. I remembered his mother looking not too unlike him in her younger days.

The two families had met in Tanzania decades

ago when their children were still in grade school. After school the children played together, often on the beach, while the parents, after work, played tennis in the Gym Khanna Club. They made sandcastles, snorkeled and looked for sea-shells, while the grown-ups chased tennis balls, looked for golf balls in the rough and downed gimlets and punches at the bar. They were in their prime then, and life was good. Now they are struggling to keep their weakening bodies together as well as they can.

"Let me in Mom, let me in." he cried.

"Will, what are you doing here?" she asked her son incredulously, "Didn't I tell you not to come down? The wind is far too strong and waves dangerously high. And where in the name of God is the coat that I gave you for Xmas, you'll be a block of ice before long." She shook her head as he stepped into the room and gave his mother a bear hug which almost knocked her down. She was not too steady on her feet these days.

"Ah, that was when I knew I had to come down, the waves will be terrific, I cannot miss this opportunity of riding one of them in a hurricane in Virginia!" so saying, he plonked down his gear and took a look at all of us,

"Well Mom, you have quite a house full here," turning to us, he yelled, "So, hurry up and eat your stew, who will come with me?" They all jumped up immediately, rushed to get on their bathing costumes and were ready. The two grandmothers did not budge, Nora's own mother used the excuse that she had to stay with her youngest, who obviously could not go. The septuagenarians could only shake their heads in dismay and weakly said,

"Be careful, and, do look out for the younger girls."

"Come on Mom, of course we will, you know we are all good swimmers." Like the hurricane they all rushed out of the house in one 'whoosh.'

Nature against Nature – the STORM

The sky was overcast and there was a deathly calm and silence, the leaves on the highest branches of the mango trees were still, even the large palm tree leaves, which moved at the slightest breath of air, drooped and were as if dead. Mysteriously and quietly all the birds seem to have disappeared, and the stream coursing through the village, a source of fish, crabs and endless fascination for the village children, had lost all its inhabitants. What was happening, the villagers were mystified, it seemed as if the entire world had come to a standstill, waiting, watching for some dreadful event. Suddenly, a little five-year old girl shouted, very agitatedly,

"Mummy, Daddy," her deep green eyes speckled with gold were large and dark and deep. You knew you were in the presence of an old soul. Her parents often wondered what was it that made them deserve such a wonderful little creature.

"How we get such a precious little one?" her mother often wondered to herself. She and her husband had almost given up hope to ever have a child, then one day they were blessed. Life was never the same since she came into their lives. The birthing was the easiest thing, unlike what she had been warned by her own mother and friends who already were mothers of several children. It was as if the little one came out on her own, and instead of a cry she arrived with a symphony of giggles. At first, she and her husband and family were frightened, thinking an evil spirit had come into their midst. The parents approached the village priest, the Sanyasi, to come and drive out whatever evil or ghost the baby was harboring. The holy man cautiously entered the little mud hut and peered down at the newborn, who was happily sleeping on a mat made out of palm fronds, took a step back, he stared and nodded his head in amazement, chanted,

"Ram, Ram, harrey Ram," and beamed from ear to ear, then turning to the parent he had said, "You are the most fortunate couple in our village, this baby, though she is only a girl will save all the people in our village one day." He continued to stare at the little one, smiling and shaking his head from side to side in the typical Indian way when they are happy and content. Coming out of her reverie, the mother heeded to her child,

"What is it, meri jhan, (my life). Why are you so agitated? What has upset you so, you who are so happy and full of song all the time, what has made you so worried?"

"Quickly, quickly, Amma, Appa, we must go to the forest of big trees in the mountain. Now! Now! Now! Hurry up." She cried impatiently at her parents who did not seem to believe nor understand the disaster that was staring at her directly.

"Why, whatever for sweetie," said her father gently, "there is a storm coming, that's all, and we must shut our house and secure our animals. We have done this scores of times a year, this is not different."

"No Appa, this time it is not the same, come we must leave."

"How do you know?" asked her mother, trying to understand.

"Because, hmmm, because, the birds and deer have told me. The water will rise up and swallow us all if we don't hurry."

Looking at his wife worriedly, her husband whispered, "We must take her to the sanyasi, this kind of talk is increasing. Her fantasies are taking over her whole thinking."

"They are already leaving," said the little girl getting agitated, "Even the fishes are swimming out into the far deep ocean. Let's go now or we will all drown, or be killed by all sorts of stuff flying in the air..."

"What are you talking about, my darling, stuff flying in the air?" "Mummy, Daddy, why don't you listen to me, we must go now, the stuff in people's houses: tables, chairs, beds, roofs, windows, cars, trucks, everything."

Outside, the wind began to pick up, and within no time, it began to screech and howl as things began to be blown about. A titanium grey cast filled the atmosphere and clouds as black as soot rushed across the firmament. Suddenly a blinding streak of lightning and deafening roll of thunder as if on key, ordered the sky to do a somersault and dumped all the rain onto the earth. Then came ear-drum splitting trumpeting's—-

"Our elephants, they have gone mad," the husband shouted. They grabbed their little girl and rushed out, indeed, the village elephants, who had never broken out of their thick chain shackles, were now charging madly through the village knocking down houses, herding their terrified occupants onto the streets.

"Quickly," cried the green-eyed girl, "Follow the elephants."

Everyone was screaming and shouting and calling out names of loved ones, for they had thought their beloved working elephants and old friends had suddenly, and inexplicably gone insane. But the huge pachyderms continued to usher and push people in front of them towards the big forest on the mountains. One large matriarch scooped up the girl and with her mighty trunk swung her up and placed her gently onto her back behind her ears. The mother turned and looked back out at their familiar ocean shore, the sight that met her eyes filled her with a dread so deep and terrifying, down through the soles of her feet into mother earth and more, all the water had left, exposing the ancient sands and solid earth that were the ancient beds of all that water. Crabs and fish that were not large or strong enough to swim farther out, struggled to join the others, out in the far waters where dolphins, like the elephants, were herding smaller fishes ahead of them into deeper waters. It was, though a terrifying sight, also miraculous: it was not "every man for himself," it was all able animals for other less able ones. The sight made the mother weep to see such humanity, or could we call it such, because these are animals, "would we do the same?" she wondered.

The elephants continued to push the terrified and befuddled villagers towards the forests. Once there, they slowed down, They, then realized what their beloved elephants were trying to do and knelt down before them and paid obeisance to their saviors.

While they were still on their knees, they did not realize what was happening behind them on the shore. The waters had retreated far enough, it then rose like a one gargantuan hungry water-mountain and began to rush towards the shore, taller than the coconut palms, taller than the mango trees and even taller than those new multistoried buildings further inland. The loud screams emanating from the human throats were no match for the totally deafening roar of the water-mountain, followed by the most powerful crashing sounds perhaps like cities blocks continually crashing down at the same moment. The wind, as if competing with the rising, rushing and crashing waters also rose in decibels and speed. Like match- sticks, houses were smashed, the storm saw no difference whether they were made of mud or concrete. "tables and chairs and beds, cars, trucks" as their little daughter had predicted, were blown and carried away into the air and dumped, hither and thither, hopefully not over some poor human or animal. The lucky ones, due to their elephants, were on high ground, the forest offered some resistance to the onslaught. The villagers could only stand and watch the biblical disaster happen before them. The elephants meanwhile had formed a tight ring right around their owners and master – or is it the other way around? The villagers sat down and chanted various mantras and waited till Mother Nature was satisfied with her punishment, there was nothing they could do, just to wait. In all this madness, people clung onto to tree branches, climbed up on their roofs, some even tried to swim against the on rushing waters, sooner more than later, most of them had to give in to Mother Nature's wrath and be swallowed by her. Bodies began to float by, some with astonished expressions on their faces, others of horror and some with resignation. Some were crushed by falling man-made debris. All these unfortunate souls were deposited here and there strewn about like all the bricks and sticks, concrete and metal – discarded and useless.

It must have been hours that they were sitting and chanting, then they realized, their elephants had already scattered and were calmly munching on the green debris around them. They were obviously not frightened nor tense any more. Sitting on the largest matriarch was the green-eyed little girl, she looked around for her parents. When she found them, the elephant bent her huge trunk around for her to stand on and gently lowered down to them. The little girl hugged her savior's huge left front leg and ran up to her parents, who were speechless with joy and gratitude.

After some more time had passed, and the rest of the villagers realized that it was all over, people began to wander about the debris and smashed houses, picking up this or that and throwing them down again. There was nothing to salvage, the devastation was total, the only thing to do was to start anew. The Gods are angry with us, we must do something to appease them, they all agreed. But what? Meanwhile, the village elders decided that they must first of all clean up the mess and rebuild their mud huts, pick up the metal utensils that can be salvaged and sweep the grounds of glass and other dangerous debris. It will take weeks and months, maybe even years before things will be back to 'normal' again. So, a little bit at a time, the villagers began to pile unwanted debris in one area, and reusable kitchen utensils and furniture in another, and lumber in a third. The women made a makeshift outdoor kitchen and picked edible greens, there was a plethora of coconuts, gathered fish and shell fish off the beaches and kept several large kettles of stew going while the men worked at cleaning their environment. While all this was going on, the children, being children played and sang and recited what they had learnt in school. The Little green-eyed girl watched quietly from a distance, sometimes going up to her mother to whisper something in her ear, but always returned to her beloved friend the elephant, which she names 'Shanti' and sat between her two huge trunk-like legs. At times she would sit on Shanti's curled trunk and she would be lulled to sleep in it like a cradle. Throughout, she did not say or do much, at times one could hear her hum an unknown tune in time with the swinging of the trunk and at times she would jump down and go to the sea shore to pick up something she had gleaned when sitting on top of her friend. She did not seem to eat anything, nor want for anything at all. This worried her mother a bit, but her father simply said,

"What do you expect, she is only a child, and children are often very picky about what they eat."

The cleaning, reparation and rebuilding continued for many weeks, but gradually things began to take on a more 'normal' look. The temple, had but minor damages, was one of the few buildings, which survived the onslaught of Mother Nature. It was the only structure in the village not built of mud and wattle. The villagers had come together many years ago, collected enough money to buy concrete blocks from a builder, and with the help of him and his crew, had built this small temple to Shiva, God of Destruction. They had even rented a sander and polished the floor of the main meeting room, so that it was shiny and smooth underfoot. Someone from the town had donated a handsome statue of Shiva in his Dance of Destruction pose. He was a handsome statue and well loved, as one can tell by the fine patina on his shoulders and uplifted knee and big toe of his right leg.

Throughout all these difficult days, weeks and months, the little girl wandered about the reconstructions of her village looking at this and that, chatting to the villagers, and smiling at them, not so much encouraging or giving advice, but simply to put smiles on their faces too as she walked by singing softly. She was quite often followed by most of the children, even the older ones. If one of them fell, scraped a knee or walked into a low beam before it was raised, she would run to them and offer help; or if some adults could not agree on something, or got into argument and maybe even fist fights, she was right there. They would look at her smile and feel ashamed of themselves and get back to work. There was nothing she could not put right simply by her presence. The village elder, who used to have the eyes and ears of the villagers, now began to feel redundant, and slowly, without realizing it, a creeping resentment began to rise up in him. He could not look at the little one without feeling angry and irritable. He tried to intervene in disputes several times, only to be told "Let us see what Maya has to say." Of course, she usually did not have to say anything, for the minute they were in her presence, all disagreements would miraculously vanish, the offending parties would shake their "Indian head-shake" smile and be on their way. The poor village elder would bow his head in shame, the resentment building up slowly but surely in his now blackening heart.

At last, on one fine day, all seem to be done and there were no more debris anywhere, most of the mud huts were rebuilt and all the dirt foot paths were swept and clean of dangerous obstacles. The village elders had called a meeting in the main shed, which also doubled as the market place on week-ends.

When everyone had gathered, the village chief announced,

"We have been very fortunate that no one lost their lives in our village, and we have little Maya and her elephant friends to thank. She is indeed a blessed of the gods."

Everyone smiled at Maya's parents, nodded and mumbled in agreement, and shook their 'Indian-head-shakes.'

"Before we began our work," continued the Village Chief, "I had said that we must offer a sacrifice to our Lord Shiva for protecting us. Now the time has come......." Before he had finished, the Sanyasi rushed in from his mat under the single still standing mango tree, for this was his 'home', this is where he meditated, ate whatever food the villagers were kind enough to share with him, and slept at night covered only with a thin cotton cloth someone, years ago, had left for him on his mat.

"Nay, nay," he shouted from outside, "This cannot be..." but before he had finished his sentence, the Village Chief's words could be heard loud and clear.

"To offer to our Lord the most precious possession we own in our small village," he stopped and looked around at everyone, then shouted, "Maya!"

Not even the waves crashing on the beach could be heard, there was dead silence, every man, woman and child's face had turned to stone. No one breathed, no one moved. The birds in the air disappeared again, the sun seemed to be darkened by an inexplicable black cloud. Time stood still for a moment. Then all hell broke loose again, and this time by the elephants.

They came charging towards the meeting shed and headed straight for the Village Chief, who cowed, shivering and sniveling and tried to crawl under the makeshift table he was sitting behind. His words might have sounded good, but the intention was certainly NOT. Suddenly, out of nowhere, Maya stood in front of the matriarch of the herd.

"No, Shanti, you must not, he is not worth your wrath. Please forgive him." Shanti already had her trunk raised and was about to bring it crashing down on the table and crush everything on and under it. She stopped, looked at Maya, turned and without a sound left. She was hurt. Maya ran after her "Shanti, please, Shanti, Shanti." But she disappeared into the forest. Maya sat down on the ground and sobbed. Her parents came to her and sat down with her,

"Maya," said her mother softly, "Shanti will come back, I am sure. She loves you too much."

"Amma, I have hurt my Shanti, she was only trying to protect me. But Amma, my time has come, I must leave soon."

"What do you mean? Leave this meeting? Run away so the Village Chief cannot get you?"

Maya shook her head and look down. "No Amma, leave you and Appa.

Leave this village. My work is done here, and my time has come."

"Leave soon, leave us, leave this village, what are you talking about, are you not our child? What do you mean, 'your time has come,' and what work are you talking about?" She was totally confused, saddened and distressed. Then she called to her husband, "Hey," (Indians did not address their husbands by their names) "Maya said she is going to leave us!" Having mouthed those words, she could not stem her sobs. She cried, hit her own forehead, rocked back and forth, for she just could not grasp the meaning of all this. "What have we done to her, did we harm her in any way that she has decided to leave us? She has been the joy of our lives, 'mera Jhan' (our Life), our reason for living."

Her husband took his wife and daughter in his arms and hugged them tightly.

"Soonyeh, (listen), woman of my house (Indian men did not call their wives by their names either) Maya has always been very special, we never did understand her abilities and saintliness, perhaps she was loaned to us by Lord Shiva to save us from certain death. We must try to understand. Now that we are all safe and our lives back to normal, we must return Maya to whomsoever had sent her to us." Then he too burst into tears.

Maya, who had quietened down, looked at her father and nodded.

"Yes Appa, I must now leave, I have other duties elsewhere. But I will come by now and then to check on you both." So, saying, she all of a sudden lifted into the air, all her parents could see was a magical golden colored bird soaring high above the clouds. They looked up in wonder. The villagers saw that too, knelt down on the ground and several times touched their foreheads in the dirt in unison.

From time to time it is said that a golden bird was seen to glide over the village, and every time it did so, the matriarch elephant trumpeted and flapped her ears.

Night Vs Day

She had been up the whole night helping her pottery-mates fire a woodfired kiln. It was quite magical as they sat around the large kiln spouting sparkled orange and red flames high into the night sky. New Delhi was very hot during the summer months, so they always fired at night, even then it was almost unbearable to sit in front of the fire breathing 'dragon.' Some kind souls kept the potters hydrated with bottles of mineral water, and hot sweet tea, which was always welcome in spite of those hot conditions. Her husband felt sorry for those hard-working potters and brought them samosas, dahl-puris (chick-pea pancakes) and other delicious fingers snacks. Yet others kept everyone awake and amused with guitar and songs, so all in all it was quite a "party." The hardship was just a side effect.

Guruji (master) said that they must check the thermostat to make sure that they reach 2100 Celsius before shutting down the kiln. It was hardest during the last hours or two because it was relatively quick for the kiln to reach 1900 to 2000 degree Celsius, but the last couple of hundred degrees took much more blood, sweat and perseverance to reach. During the last hour, one at a time an 8" x 2" piece of hardwood, must be thrown into each of the fire boxes on either side of the kiln. The person on the right of the kiln would throw one in and shout, "done." Then the person on the other side responded, threw one into his fire-box and shouted in reply, "Done," and so on. Meanwhile Guruji sat and watched the flame-spouting chimney and waited for the color to change. As soon as the flame turned white, he shouted, "We have reached temperature." A triumphant yell went up to join the flame,

"Yippee!! It is white, we have reached temperature." But to make certain that this was true, the weary potters still had to look through removeable plugged-up peep-holes into the kiln to see that the thermostat, three-inch long pyramids which was made with the same clay as the pottery, has bent over; if the vertical clay thermostat were bent to almost a ninety degree angle, then the kiln had reached the required temperature. Quickly, the fire boxes were closed, and all other openings sealed with clods of moist clay.

Unbeknownst to them, it was already daylight

when everything was sealed and the area around the kiln swept, the tables were set up to receive the fired ware. Stools and chairs put in strategic places around Guruji's chair so that he could critique each pot as they were removed from the kiln, which has to be left to cool slowly, about twenty-four hours or so before it was opened, because if it was opened too soon the sudden temperature change may cause many pots to crack. Many impatient 'green potters' often learned the hard way.

She dragged herself to the large living room with a domed ceiling, of Guruji's house, and collapsed on the cool tiled floor and was instantly asleep. While she was lying there, one of the potters awakened her,

"There is a phone for you." She opened her eyes.

"Oh My God, I forgot, I was supposed to be the guest of honor in the XinLing Ambassador's residence for a 'Welcome to New Delhi' coffee morning."

"Hello," as she warily picked up the phone, "This is she,"

"Where are you? We are all waiting for you. You were supposed to be here at 10 am. I sent the driver for you, but they could not find you at home."

"Oh, I am so sorry, I was in the pottery studio firing a kiln all night, we just finished. It was quite an experience. Wonderful."

"Madam, can you come now? We are all waiting, you are the guest of honor!" The social secretary sounded a bit miffed.

"I will have to go home and get cleaned up and changed............" But before she could finish, she was interrupted,

"You can come as you are, it doesn't really matter." Now she sounded annoyed.

"But you don't understand, we have been firing all night, there is soot in my hair, I am wearing my old kurta/pajamas............."

"It will be alright, just wash your face and come."

"Alright, if you say so." She replied and smiled a secret smile with glee. Let us shock those 'fancy' ladies, as one of her Indian artist friends called the Foreign Service wives. She hung up the phone and turned to her fellow potters, all stained, dirty and soot in the hair and eyelashes,

"Well, ladies and gentlemen, I am going to

have 'morning coffee' with some fancy ladies in the XinLing Ambassador's residence."

"Can we come?" Someone implored, they serve the best momos (meat dumplings) in town, and as for the coffee," "Do they even serve coffee?" "I don't think so, but they do have salted tea." She replied.

"Oh no, salted tea? Must be awful,"

"They mix yak's milk and salt into the tea, then it is churned forever into a frothy mixture. Quite palatable when one finally gets used to the idea of drinking salty-milky tea."

"I still don't think I will ever grow to like it," said one lady pulling a face. "I wish you all could come, but I think I am in my social secretary's bad books already."

"How so, what do you mean, we all love you."

"Well, I do not like shopping, I wear Indian outfits, I shop in the local market myself rather than tell my cook to do the shopping. I love to go to Old Delhi and eat street foods, but what is worst is, I am always hanging out with you lot crazy artists."

"Ha ha," they laughed, "Then you better get along."

Then she twirled around them, made a deep

curtsy, beamed her 'million-dollar' smile, and said, "How do I look?"

"Fantastic!"

By that time, the company car had arrived and was waiting for her in the shade of the large Neem tree, under whose great canopy were eight kick-wheels. This magnificent tree was also the home for a pair of peacocks and a small flock of crows. Much that they loved the peacocks, they were a menace to the potters, because they would sit on the branches above and without warning decide to irrigate the land once in a while. Being rather larger birds, it was not a pleasant experience. They considered moving the wheels, but the heat was more unbearable than the occasional showering. Actually, the crows were more annoying, being more intelligent, they were also curious, they would swoop down and land, just out of reach, on one of the unused wheels, stand on the wheel-head and observe us. They tilted their heads this way and that, and on a whim would suddenly fly up and land on a newly made pot, which of course, immediately collapsed. The surprised bird would flap its wings lift up and caw with dismay, then when it landed on something solid, would turn and look at the potter accusatively as if to say,

"You did that, you, stupid human." It then

flew to higher branches and continue to caw to his mates, together they would make quite a cacophony.

She drove off in the white Mercedes Benz. If the driver noticed anything odd about his 'memsahib,' he was not going to show it. It seems because of her quirkiness and non-conformity, she was well like and admired by all the staff. They left the mundane section of New Delhi, and entered the spacious, quite streets of Embassy row. Most of the Residences, as they were called, were on very large compounds surrounded by high walls of brick or stone, often topped by broken glass. There were armed guards by the front gates, some even had small kiosks to keep the guards from the weather. All very nice and 'civilized.'

They pulled up into the XinLing Residence, the armed guard came up to the car and spoke to the driver. The gate was opened, and we glided into the compound. They had left the noise, confusion and congestion of India outside. It was her first time in India, and all this seemed quite strange and unnatural to her. She felt as if she had entered a land-bound ocean liner surrounded by manicured lawns, dotted with well-tended garden beds and sharply edged walkways and garden paths. It was the silence that was the most surprising thing about these residences. Outside their gated walls one could almost not hear oneself think.

They stopped in front of a small cottage adjacent to the main building. The driver seemed to know exactly where the she was supposed to be. He got out of the car and opened the door for her. As she got out of the car, her social secretary dressed immaculately in a lavender saree with matching sandals was waiting for her. On her left arm were her signature multi-banded bangles; her ears were ornamented with long multitiered amethyst earrings, and there were rings on three of her fingers of each hand. She was a slightly rotund well-presented upper-middle class educated Indian memsahib. She approached her own Memsahib, looked at her, without batting and eye "Madam, this way please," and led her through a rather ornate door into a very pleasant anti-room all decked out in white and off-white colors. After a very brief hesitation, she opened the door into the Sun-room of the little 'Summer Cottage."

"Ladies. Let me introduce Mrs. Prismith. She is the wife of our new Res-Rep of the International Bank. This is their first India assignment. They arrive short of six months ago, and as you see,

Mrs. Presmith is already well acquainted with our city." She looked her up and down, smiled and sat down.

Mrs. Prismith looked around the very pretty room, with many large windows, draped with gauzy white on white printed floor to ceiling curtains. Wicker furniture, painted in a very tasteful very light green, the color of baby sprouts, were arranged in threes and fours of "conversation groups."

Small round matching wicker tables were interspersed here and there, on which glasses of white and rose wine and dainty finger foods were placed. She stood at one end of the gracious room, looked at everyone and smiled. She had to exercise great restraint not to giggle at the shocked expressions on their faces They did not know what to make of this 'raggamuffin' of the International Bank First Lady.

"Ahem," she began, "I'm sure you are wondering if perhaps Mrs. Shah," she said, pointing to her Social Secretary, "has made a mistake, alas she has not, I am she who Mrs. Shah says I am, and you all will have to accept me as you see me." She looked around again, seeing Mrs. Shah raise her eyebrow, looked down on the floor, and probably wished it would open up and swallow her. "You see, I genuinely forgot about this little gathering. I was firing a kiln all night, a very exhausting though exhilarating activity, so I was completely tired out and crashed on my guruji's floor and fell asleep."

"What were you doing?" asked one of the ladies, "Firing, what do you mean?" This got the attention of the gathering, for they started to whisper among each other......

"Oh, let me explain. I am a potter, and some of us have made some pottery and were firing them, ie. To cure them in an oven, called a kiln, so that they can be glazed and used as table ware, vases and other functional containers."

"We must place each pot into the kiln, when the kiln is full, we must close it and start a fire in the fire boxes. It takes many kilos of small 8" x 2" pieces of hard wood. All this done by hand for hours and hours. Once the temperature rises, we cannot stop, we cannot let it drop or we would have to start all over again. This is why we get all excited and exhausted at the same time."

"Oh, wow, how interesting."

"So, you are a potter," said another, "How long have you been a potter?"

"I just started here shortly after we arrived

here. You see, one of my friends in Washington DC had some beautiful blue pottery, which they used as their dinner service; I asked them from where had they purchased those plates and bowls."

"Aren't they beautiful," the wife answered, "I fell in love with them the moment I saw them. When we were in New Delhi, we saw them in this pottery studio, called Delhi Blue, off the Ring Road, went in and we completely fell in love with Mr. Singh's pottery and bought a complete dinner set."

"I know Delhi Blue," chimed in another lady, "In fact I have one or two pieces by them."

"Yes, that was where I was all night, till I was awakened and brought here, as I am. You see, when I heard that my husband was to be sent to New Delhi, I immediately decided that I would take up pottery when we came.

Now that our sea freight has arrived, and we are all unpacked and settled down, I sought out Delhi Blue and came and asked GuruJi Singh to take me on as one of his students. I have never been happier."

She glanced over at her Social Secretary, who at last began to smile a bit, and breathed a sigh of relief, she was relieved that her 'Memsahib' did not make a fool of herself, on the contrary, all the ladies were full of questions and eager to visit that Pottery Studio. They seemed to have forgotten her disheveled state, and her clay stained kurta-pajamas.

"I'll tell you what, the kiln will be opened the day after tomorrow, please come for the opening. It is quite an exciting 'happening.' I promise, you all will be pleasantly surprised." We will have beer, snacks and maybe even Champaign, if someone will bring a bottle or two?" This was greeted with applause and declarations of;

"I will bring a couple," volunteered one lady,

"And I will too," said another. Before one could count, at least a dozen ladies had volunteered.

"I will be definitely be there," and "I can hardly wait," and "Maybe I will also become a student of Guruji Singh."

Then everyone started to talk to together and ask me dozens of questions. "Where do you get the clay,"

"Well, unlike the States, we can buy it in 25lb boxes, we have to go to the mountain-sides and dig it up ourselves."

"Oh no, I will never be able to do that." Exclaimed one of the ladies, "Sorry, Mary, I was just teasing, it is true we have to dig up our own clay, but you and I do not have to do it. It is the workmen's job."

"Phew," breathed one of the new prospective new students.

While we were still chatting animatedly, lunch was announced. We all went into a small, again taste-fully decorated dining room, in hints of pink and white. Mrs. Prismith excused herself and went into the ladies' room. In the waiting area was a most comfortable chaise lounge – she laid down "just only for a minute" she said to herself, but the minute her head and body was supine, she was away.

The ladies in the dining room waited, and finally Mrs. Shah and Mary, got up to check what was the matter, they found her fast asleep. Mary said, "Let her sleep."

To the others they said, "She is dead to the world, so we decided to let her sleep. She deserves it."

Dawu-One Hundred Years Later

The surrounding mountains grew taller as we left the new metropolis of Chengdu, Sichuan, but the super highway we were on were as wide and smooth as any in my adoptive homeland of this country, USA. However, not only did the mountains grew in height, they seemed to be closing in on us ever so gradually that I did not notice, because I was distracted and impressed at the dense vegetation around us, and on closer inspection, I saw that in among the trees, shrubs, the empty spaces along the super highways and any, what we would consider in our country as 'waste' land there were healthy vegetables growing in abundance. I did not recognize them, but they looked delicious. Then I noticed the first of the numerous tunnels we were to go through, because the mountains had become too steep and close, construction of highways became almost impossible, so the solution? Burrow through them. At first, I started to count them, as we went through, and kept an eye on the length, soon I lost count at a dozen or more, and the length varied from 5 to 50 kilometers. Later, on the other side of the chain, we were to encounter even more. Some of these long tunnels had been ingeniously installed with arched reflectors following the semicircle of the tunnels themselves, so as we entered they lit up very brightly as if with artificial bands of electrical lights; on the ground were, of course the universal 'cats-eyes' Quite a saving of electricity.

We had also been gradually rising in elevation, and our guide passed around 'high altitude candies' for those of us who might not be able to tolerate it. By the time we reached out first destination, Ya'an, we peaked at about 4,000', the surroundings peaks were between 5,000 to almost 8,000' feet.

As we approached Khangding, the mountains really began to close in on us and we had to descend to be closer to the now ever increasingly rushing river which rages through the town center, what was once a small town where my father went to Middle School. In those days, the Khangding Love song was known and sung by everyone, and I was happy to hear it as we neared it just like my father used to sing to me as a wee girl. This river used to be so loud that one could not make a normal conversation with someone standing beside you, but nowadays, it has to compete with all the noise making devises of 'prosperity' we call "progress." I think it is holding its own very well. However, when I was awakened early next morning, I thought we were in a heavy rain storm, I opened the window and looked out, but there was no storm, in fact a rather clear blue sky, there were few cars on the road and there, 13 floors below us was the river in it old glory. I was satisfied that it is still the landmark all residents and visitors look to. Alas! it is still used as a suicide vehicle, because once you jumped/fell in there is no return.

The next day, we drove out of Khangding and headed for Dawu, my father birth place, now known as Dafu, the valley opened up when we reached the outskirts, I saw a large developments of housing estates, other enterprises and small businesses at the edge of a large mountain lake, I asked our guide what was that, he looked at me proudly,

"The government is building small apartments to house 30,000 people, this will be the New Khangding, just as Shanghai has its New City, Pudong, and Chengdu has its New City, so Khanding will also. You will also notice that on every house there is a tubular structure with a continuous elongated winding pipe – those are solar powered water storage-units which will provide each three-bed room house with hot water. He looked at me pointedly and paused, I could almost see his chest swell with pride.

Then we continued along the two-lane winding road towards Dawu.

I was both excited and apprehensive, and a heavy melancholy began to settle in my heart. I was sad my father did not live to see this day. The brilliant high-altitude sunshine turned into a drizzle, and out of Khangding valley, turned into a mild rain, I had hoped to see the sun glint on the sacred Mountain peak of Nichi La, my father had spoken of, which watched over Dawu, but, I then concluded in my heart that this was his tears, sad that he could not be with me, but happy that I was able to make this difficult trek to this remote place.

As we neared the Dawu, it was no longer the one dirt road little village of few hundred people, of course, it is exactly one hundred years since that infant's loud voice broke the silence of the valley with his cry, and now my own tear fell silently. It had become quite a prosperous town, not the size of Khangding, but sizeable enough, as it is now the center of agricultural and environmental research. That is why we saw so many herds of yaks, and large organized ploughed fields, at least not by our American standards to be sure, since many are still worked by farm animals and humans. As we approached Dawu, suddenly the name Gokah popped into my vision, it was the village my Grandfather's batman, Yang TsanCheng, had retired to when he left his services just before Grandpa was transferred to Chengdu. Yang had inherited a small yak farm of about twenty-five heads, plus a few horses my Grandpa had given him. His wife and sons were waiting for him after all those years of following my Grandpa. I had imagined in my mind's eye a wind-blown village with scant mud-brick houses scattered among the meadows and lowlands each one guarded by the fierce-some Tibetan mastiff on a large chain; these animals, often called 'lion-dogs' because of their large main surrounding their large heads. They will kill any intruders without restraint. What I found now, was a small thriving town painted colorfully in primary colors, two storied cement-block houses, richly decorated window "treatments" on the outside. They were no longer the traditional Khamba dwellings, where the animals lived on the ground floor and people on the first, with flat roofs for drying vegetables and bedding and clothing, and a small front and back courtyard. All these houses still had front courtyards rich with fruit trees and vegetable, and all around the houses were surrounded by man high walls. The animals were allowed to roam free. The town was clean and the streets well swept, if not by brooms, at least by the frequent rains. After a couple of photos ops., we continue my pilgrimage.

Dawu came upon us gradually, our very modern driver was following his GPS on this smart phone and all of a sudden, we stopped in front of the one and only hotel in town, be it 3 or 4 or 5 stars, we had no choice. But it was new, grand and constructed in the old Tibetan style: heavy solid wooden furniture intricately carved and furnished with embroidered cushions and coverlets. I wondered where had they acquired the hardwood, as we did not see many dense forests in this valley.

Our rooms were on the third floor. At the front desk two slight young girls, dressed in Tibetan gowns, simply tucked their skirts into their waists, to reveal modern and stylish cut-up jeans and trainers, they picked up our heavy bags and trotted up the stairs. Our rooms were small, rendered even smaller by the large heavy furniture, one almost had to climb over the huge chairs in order to get to the beds or windows. However, the bedding was luscious and inviting. We, being old, one octogenarian, two septuagenarians and only one around 50, had a difficult time contemplating the descent to the dining room two flights down steep stairs and back up again! We did go and it was worth every morsel. The dining room was separated into private cubicals, this too was designed and constructed by the owner, his wife did all the interior decoration with tasteful Buddhist figures and mythologies. During the diner, the mother of the architect came to meet us. she did not know any English, but could understand Mandarin and spoke it with a Tibetan accent. My good friend, the organizer of this adventure and I asked her about my father's family and house, the original road of this town, and also the catholic church whose English priest had taught my father English; she knew that road, but, with her smart phone, she consulted her friend about my father's family house and the church. We were told that all the old houses were either destroyed by numerous earthquakes, or, were torn down when the government came through to help the residents build newer, better and more permanent ones.

Our breakfast was freshly made Chinese Congee rice with various condiments all grown nearby and freshly made by the cook. The whole business was run by one joint family. As pre-arranged at dinner, we met the owner's mother after breakfast, so that she could take us to the original road. In fact, it was still the Main street of the town. As I walked along it, it was difficult to imagine my 7-year-old father running up and down this 'dirt' road with his playmates and getting into some mischief or other. It would be difficult today because most of the houses are behind high walls. The elderly lady first took us to the new church, to ask for the whereabouts of the old one, but after many minutes of knocking and shouting politely into the 'darkened' rooms, no one responded, all we heard were loud chanting's. It certainly did not sound very western, in fact I would have thought they were doing Buddhist chanting. We left and went to meet another friend of the lady, who knew where the old church was. After a hard 'slog' up the hill for us sea-level dwellers, we arrived at a high locked metal gate, but going to the side of the gate we found another smaller door through which we walked and there was an obviously European church – the long wide nave, the long and Norman-arched windows, the peaked roof and the big welcoming door. There was no steeple nor cross atop. I could almost hear Father Cunningham inviting me in, "Come, let me tell you about your father, he was......." but the sound of my sobbing took over. We were not allowed enter because it was in the process of being demolished.

The other lady invited us into her house, a highly and colorfully decorated living room with kitchen on one side. She offered us green tea and peeled and cut-up wedges of apples from her own tree under which we had sat in the front courtyard. We exchanged emails in our smart phones and promises were made. She loaded us with apples from her tree and took many photos with us. It was rare for them to see any foreigner, let alone ones from so far away as Washington DC, they had heard of that city.

The drizzle had stopped, and we walked back in silence, the lady appreciated my silence and only pointed out the "hardware" shop her second son owned and ran. She was one proud mother. At the hotel, we all bade farewell again, hugged and almost everyone cried.

1917 was my father born,

2017 for the first time, his first-born returns;

They invited me to return-

Alas, this is certainly "A Bridge Too Far."

The Last Rendezvous

After asking around in the lodge, she discovered that one of the guests, a 'white father' was also leaving that morning and would gladly give her a ride to the Serengeti Game Reserve. She was all packed and waiting in the lobby, when a rather handsome young man, in a long white priest's uniform approached her. He had a mass of ginger hair, and seemed to be in his early to mid-thirties, he came up to her, nodded, smiled and introduced himself as Father Farrell,

"You are Mrs. Walker, I see you are ready? Sorry to keep you waiting, we will leave in half an hour from now, is that alright with you?"

She was rather taken aback, for she had imagined that all white fathers were stout, grey-haired and smelled of whiskey. But this man was about her age, slim, clear browed with a pair of glinting green eyes.

"OH yes, father, I am ready. I shall wait here, where is your car?" "Just that old black van by the gates, I'll see you there."

"OK Father." She finished her cup of coffee and headed for the van. AS she approached the vehicle, she saw that he was already and putting his luggage into the back seat.

"Hey, is that all you have? For a woman of the world you do travel lightly."

"Yes, the only way I know. I like to be able to carry my own bags and go. I'm deathly afraid of porters and the like, never know where they will take my bags to nor how much to pay them," she joked.

"Right, you sit up here by me. I just have to drop this kid in his village on the way."

She threw her suitcase and sleeping bag into the back of the van and climbed in to the front seat. The child must not have been more than seven years old, who's blue black face cracked into a broad grin to reveal a set of the most beautiful white teeth.

"Hey, Jambo mtoto, what is your name?"

"Mzuri mama, mzuri sana (very well), my name is Abdullah."

"Hey, where did you learn English, you speak it very well."

"This Bwana (mister) Father is my teacher,

and I am sad he is leaving us."

"Come, come and sit down here, Father Farrell is ready to go."

"Thank you, but I must get my present for my mother. Please wait for one minute."

Off he dashed and not a moment later, returned clutching a clucking, protesting hen by its feet.

"Mtoto, (little boy) what do you have there? Where did you get that chicken?"

"It is a zawadi (gift) for mother. My uncle, the big cook in the Lodge, gave it to me."

"Hey that is good, your mother will be very happy."

"OK, let's go," shouted Father Farrell.

She turned and saw her husband on the top step in front of the main entrance to the Lodge, an anxious expression on his face, he waved wanly.

"Come back soon darling. See you in Dar."

She smiled and waved back.

"Yes," she said, and thought, "I hope so, my love." It was a sad parting. They had hoped that they would solve their difficulties of late. Though they still loved each other, but somehow an inexplicable distance and silence had come between them. They had come to this lovely Game Lodge built on and around an outcrop of huge boulders to be away from Dar-es-Salam and by themselves for a few days to try and to get to the bottom of this disquiet. He was a typical English gentleman, very discrete and shy, he did not like to encroach into another's 'space' even if the other person was his wife. He would treat her with extreme politeness and consideration. She, on the other hand, was an Asian, very warm, needed physical contact, liked to argue and talk about things, was quick to laugh and shout. She was spirited and fun-loving, spontaneous and unpredictable. Qualities he had married for, but which could not handle in the long haul. After several years of marriage, it became difficult for both of them, so the politeness and cooling started. They were sad at their own changing attitudes, but they did not know how to deal with it. He retreated more and more into his work and silence, while she, who was quite popular among the 'expats,' was often sort after at parties and many social gatherings. They came to this rather isolated and little-known Game Park to be away from those crowds to talk, but they could not bring themselves to confront each other. They parted, sad on his part and frustrated on hers, and nothing was solved.

Very quickly, the travelers were down on the plains leaving the rocky outcrop, among which was hidden a luxurious safari Lodge, looking, from a distance, not more than like a pile of intimidating stones, and before long they were within sight of Abdullah's village – a collection of mud huts hidden among acacia trees and the ubiquitous cassava plants, which neither storm nor drought can damage. Only the tuberous roots were eaten, because the leafy part of the plants were poisonous. However, cassava roots, which are ground into powder and made into a stiff dough, are eaten with a thin meaty stew. They were less than nutritious, may even be detrimental to one's health if it were the only food one had. But in times of disaster and famine, it was the only thing the people could eat, because they are grown in the ground, so neither drought nor heavy weather had much effect on them.

Father Farrell and his companions had already slowed down considerably as they neared the village, because there were some people on the edge of the road gesticulating as if asking the driver of the van to stop. But before they could, they hit it – black cotton soil – in a split second the van had made a 90 degree turn and was gliding blithely sideways down the road "Oh Lord," cried F. Farrell, "this the black cotton alright. Hold tight." They proceeded to skid into the ditch.

"I'll push," she volunteered and jumped out of the car, just as F. Farrell mouthed the word "Careful." No sooner had she got out of the car, she had immediately to hang onto the car door to keep from falling, both her feet lost traction and slid under her, it was as if she was trying to skate on ice with roller skates.

"Wow, what in the world is this stuff? I cannot push this damn car with only glass to stand on." She cried.

Some of the villagers had come out of their huts and the women were hiding their mouths behind bits of cloths, but they could not hide their mirthful eyes. Finally, when the joke was over, almost the entire village came out to help the unfortunate travelers. After many buckets of sandy soil, leaves and bits of sticks, cardboard, the van was coaxed out of the black cotton. Many hands were shaken and many more "asante-sana" (thank-you) said and once more they were on their way for the Serengeti.

"What order are you?" she asked as they

settled into a comfortable speed.

"I am a Jesuit, some people call us 'White Father...'"

"But you are not old, how long have you been here?"

"Not all WFs are old, anyway, I 've only been here three years. But some of us have been here a life-time."

"Do you expect to spend a life-time here too?"

After a pause, "God willing, and if I can live that long, yes." "How admirable. Where is your mission? In Arusha?"

"No, I live in a tiny village about the same size as Abdullah's, on the shores of Lake Victoria."

"But that's miles from here."

"Yes, I'm on sick leave, I had to go to Mwanza for medical treatment, the F. Superior told me to take a couple of weeks off."

"Aside from teaching and preaching, what else do you do? What do you do for recreation for instance?"

"Oh, I swim, like everyone else in the village. The kids are some of the best swimmers I have ever seen, and some of them can skip stones on the water as many as 15 to 20 skips. I am sure they would win the gold medal if there were such a class of sport in the Olympics."

"Swim, but isn't there bilharzia (sleeping sickness caused by a snail) in Lake Victoria?"

"Sure, almost the entire village is plagued with it, but I have the good fortune of being able to go to a hospital once a year to get 'cured'."

"Then you return to your village, resume the swimming, get bilharzia, get treatment and so on and so forth. Does it not debilitate you permanently in the long run?"

"I'm sure it does, but then I will be like the rest of the villagers."

"What does that mean?"

"We become increasingly lethargic, until it overtakes us and we expire!" He looked amused as her eyes grew wider and wider with disbelief.

"Is there no permanent solution to this?"

"What else is there to do? We cannot kill all the snails in Victoria?"

She looked at this rather handsome young priest, his pale green eyes, soft and penetrating at the same time, squinting out of a strong tanned face, not yet leathery as some of the older, more weathered Caucasian expatriates tend to become. As he described his life in the remote villages, she could not help but notice now sensuous his mouth was and how sensitive his clear brow. The fact that he was a priest only made him more tantalizing. Suddenly, he turned to her caught her stare. She blushed, but, did not look away.

"Yes, as you were saying, I swim, I get bilharzia and I get treated – that is the extent of my recreation." His voice trailed off and she could sense him casting his mind back to the days before he answered his 'calling.'

Even though they had been travelling for well over three hours the landscape around them had not changed. The sun was almost at its zenith, beating down mercilessly, unencumbered by clouds or pollution, upon the already well-baked earth. Through the heat haze, herds of gazelles and wildebeests could be seen clustered here and there lazily munching on the tough savanna grass. The more curious ones looked up and stared quite unconcernedly as the van drove pass. She too stared at the hot silent landscape without really seeing anything, her mind hundreds of miles away, mesmerized by secret desires and guilt-ridden thoughts.

"Can I ever go back to him again?" She mused, and as if reading her thoughts.

"Was that your husband?"

"Yes," she answered as she was brought out of her revere.

"Will you return to him?"

"I don't know," startled by the straight forwardness of the question.

"I don't really know, but I probably will."

"He seems like a very nice man from what little I saw of him."

"Yes, he is, he is a very good man, understanding, loving and strangely enough he still loves and wants me. He has even forgiven me for what I have done."

"Forgiven you?"

"Yes Father, I have done a great and evil deed. I hurt him deeply by falling in love with another man." A hint of sarcasm crept into her voice involuntarily, "Actually I had not intended to, I was feeling some frustration towards our marriage, and also a naughty sense of adventure crept into my consciousness. He, 'X' arrived on the scene at precisely the right moment, I took the plunge."

She remembered their first afternoon together –they were both extremely shy, he apologized madly afterwards, and she hardly able to contain herself from giggling. Falling in love came naturally to them: a couple of soul-mate paired at last. It was a wonderful exhilarating six months. The discovery and subsequent banishment, was as agonizing and painful as it was wonderful. Death would have been sweet relief.

"Is this why you are taking this safari?"

"Yes, my husband thought a change might do me good, sort of remove me from temptation, you are a priest, you should understand that, and how it positively does not work. Right?"

"No, that is not entirely fair. Removed from temptation does work given sufficient time."

"Time? The magic healer or all wounds? When all pain and ecstasy is rendered numb and relegated to an inner storage chamber and can only be remembered and 'aired' every seven years or so? Look Father, you know how much misery and suffering there is in this world – I'm sure you see it even in your tiny village, and how little love exists between people, then tell me, how can it be so wrong to love and be loved by someone?"

"It is wrong only some else gets hurt."

"That's nonsense. People don't get half as hurt as their pride does. If you truly loved someone, then you should rejoice in whomsoever your love loves, and if that person truly loves you back, then she/he will not stop doing so just because she loves someone else, it just an addition that's all."

"That is too idealistic a position. People are not that self-sacrificing and self-less......"

"C'mon, you are the priest, you are the one who is supposed to teach about love and charity and all that,"

"But I am also human..."

"So, you agree that people are not perfect,"

"I did not say that."

"But let's assume that people are not, that we are ego-eccentric and selfish, and that when we love we do so from precisely that point of view; we are in fact better at being loved than loving, and in this state, we assume that we are in the 'central' position of our lover. Now, if this lover were to love some else also, what do you think happens?"

"Well..... hurt, rejection, betrayal, sadness, bitterness, and yes even anger, and finally that 'green-eyed monster' jealousy."

"You feel abandoned, deceived and a sense of outrage, you cannot understand nor accept what has happened."

"You are indignant, you are wronged."

"Yes."

"And where were those finer qualities of love? Have they in one quick move been entirely removed and replaced by all those new negative, dark emotions? Was it you who was hurt or was it really your pride of having lost your 'central' position and being replaced by another, a state of affairs the ego finds intolerable?"

"Only at first, but gradually one can accept the situation...."

"Can one? Is this why there are so may 'rebound marriages and affairs?' from one 'central' position to a new one as quickly as possible, so to speak."

"No, no, given time and distance one can get used to it."

"Is this what you have done?" she asked suddenly, detecting that she had struck the core, "Is this why you, a handsome young man with a bright future decided to run all this way?"

A slight frown darkened his face and he looked at her sadly,

"Yes, yes you are right. I was only running away. I didn't really have the true calling. This was as far, both in distance and time, as I could run. When she told me that she going to marry someone else my head exploded inside me. I could not face the rest of life without her. I experienced all those emotions we spoke about and more. I could not believe that she could love anyone else other than myself. I wanted to kill her and the other man, and I hated myself for thinking it. Then indeed I would be without her, at least not I have her in my heart and thought. Hardly a day goes by without me thinking of her. I guess this is my other form of 'recreation'."

"How long has it been since she got married?"

"It's almost four years to the day."

"And you still think about her? Incredible. However, I am sure this strong personal involvement has made a better priest of you."

"Perhaps, perhaps, I hope......"

"Oh, I am certain of it. You know what love is and what is loss. You have suffered. What clse is there to know in Life?"

They lapsed into silence, each absorbed in his and her thoughts. In the distance, the Government run game lodge came into focus – a rather modern building, surrounded clusters of permanent tents. As they neared, they could see game wardens and lodge attendants dressed smartly in green, darting about between the acacia trees and dwellings trying to busy themselves in the lazy afternoon. A few tourists heavily laden with cameras around their necks lounged about on the terrace, some peering through their binoculars scanning the wilderness in the hopes of spotting the 'one- upmanship-animal – the leopard!'

"How about some lunch?" He announced, waking her from her day dreaming.

"I'd love it, just what I've been thinking about," she said with a sly smile.

"Like hell you have! There's nothing more forceful than a swearing priest." He grinned.

They parked their van under an appropriate tree and walked over to the dining room, which was already quite full. Most of the customers seemed to be either overweight or elderly. I suppose these are the people who can afford an African safari.

"Come with me to the Ngorogoro Crator, I have two weeks of leave left." He asked her during lunch.

"I cannot, I have a train ticket back to Dar. However, it is a tempting invitation. I'll think about it. Thanks for asking."

"Do consider it, I haven't had a talk like that since I left Canada, and I do admire you very much." She smiled shyly and continued to eat her overcooked curry. After lunch, she stretched out on one of the lawn chairs, she felt less sad, somehow this White Father had relaxed her, perhaps in hearing of his story made her forget her own problems for a while, or perhaps she found in him an empathetic soul. Anyway, she soon dozed off into a gentle dreamless sleep. She awoke to find F. Farrell gazing intently at her.

"Sorry, I dozed off," she stretched luxuriously in the warmth of his gaze.

"I'm sorry, I did not mean to wake you. Now that you are awake, let us go and find us a leopard."

"Oh yes, please."

The savanna was a sea of waving gold, and in the vast emptiness even a large herd of gazelle seemed insignificant. Sometimes, as if at a signal a few would leap straight up into the air and bound away leaping and galloping causing chaos and fear. Just as suddenly they would stop and graze quietly once more as if nothing had happened. They stopped the van behind a large rocky outcrop, turned off the engine and waited. The immense silence completely enveloped them. Soon the object of the gazelle's agitation became apparent. In the not too far distance was a lioness who decided to rise from her afternoon siesta, stretched herself and slinked lazily foreword again, a few steps later, she collapsed on the ground, her distended belly and feet turned skyward – total and utter repose after a good meal. On closer scrutiny, one could see the other sandy beasts flopped about in the tall dry grass, also full of sleep and food. Even though these are the 'king of beasts,' they look no more fierce than giant pussy-cats. The desire to go up and stroke them must be curtailed. They drove on towards a stream-bed where there was a thin copse of trees, where, the game warden had said they might be able to spot a leopard or two. As they approached the main forest, they flushed out a large nervous made ostrich who fanned out his magnificent black plumes and exposed a pair of rather ugly but strong sun-burnt legs. He ran away in a flash of black, red and brown. Locating the leopard was no easy matter and they had almost given up when by chance she looked up at the yellow trunks of the acacia trees, and there cradled between two large limbs was a hulk of spotted muscles, and feet dangling ground wards. A pair of emerald green slits lazily gazed at the dumbfounded humans. They stopped the van under the culprit tree and stared in awe at this powerful animal. For several minutes, they stared at each other but for the occasional twitch of the tip of the tail, one could have mistaken it for a part of the tree itself. After a while they drove away not daring to speak for fear of breaking the primeval spell.

The golden plains were taking on a russet hue as the sun began to set. Instinctively, they looked for a 'camp site,' unlike wild animal predators, who awaken at night and prowl for preys, homo sapiens seek for shelter and rest. They came to an enormous baobab tree on which was tacked a weather-beaten small wooden sign that read 'CAMPSITE IV'

"What, is this a campsite?' she asked incredulously, and looked around her. There were no huts nor shelter of any kind, no bench, no circle of stones, nothing.

"Yes." Came the calm reply, "Yes madam!"

"I think I shall sleep in the car." He laughed and said,

"Of course you will, and so will I," seeing the worried expression on her face, added, "Well it is between the wild cats and a White Father," he teased, "Which will you chose?"

"Ha ha, don't worry, I will sleep in the back of

the van." He smiled.

"Oh sorry, I forgot you are 'preordained.'" She teased back. Then facing the solitude around her, the star-studded blackness seep into her entire being and she felt restored.

"You know Father, this is where I belong. I don't ever want to leave this savanna. I can feel my soul fly out of me and blend with all that is around me. Do you think it is possible to live here alone?"

"It is possible, I am sure, but it will be extremely difficult."

"Hey, after all, the Masai's live in the wilderness."

"Yes, but they always have and have known nothing else. Why don't you come with me to the Ngorogoro and see for yourself how they live. I will take you back to Dar in a week's time. We will go to Lake Manyara, Kilimanjaro and maybe even climb the old Kaiser mountain."

"No Father, I cannot. I must remain here for some time, I feel like a pilgrim who has at last found her shrine."

"It is not safe to stay here all by yourself. I need your companionship. Please."

"Hush," he said suddenly, "quick, get into the car now."

"What is it?" she asked,

"In the car NOW." He had heard the silent cough of leopard. While they were talking, they had not realized the gathering sounds outside. Not wanting to alarm her, he said,

"Nothing, just some big animals snorting and chomping on the grass. Go to sleep.

Maybe by the morning you will change your mind and come with me.

Good night."

She listened to the crescendo outside and thought she saw millions of shiny eyes like the sky above. Gradually she fell asleep in a mesmeric state as if she will never wake again. She heard many grunts and snorts and puffs throughout the night but thought nothing of it, thinking that she was dreaming again. The sun was still below the horizon, but already it was light and in the East the sky put on a crimson glow in readiness for the sun. She sat up and looked out of the window: and was confronted with a sight she had read about, but never in a million years did she dream that she would be in the midst of it. They were caught in the middle of the Great Animal Migration of

East Africa. They were surrounded by hundreds of thousands of wildebeests, zebras, gazelles, wild dogs, hyenas, and all manner of antelopes. They had all decided to stop at CAMP IV for the night.

Quickly and quietly she got out of the van, her heart pumping away for the sheer excitement and joy of it all. It was loving and dying all rolled into one. Without a moment's hesitation, she walked into their midst. The animals nearest stepped aside and took no notice of her. They kept on grazing and eating. The sun began to rise rapidly, then, miraculously the animals, as if on a signal, began to line themselves up into ranks and files of about 6 to 8 in a row. They began to move towards the north and east. She, too, started to walk in their direction. Yes, yes, she said to herself, as if in a delirium, I have arrived at last, this is where I belong. She was vaguely aware of the moving animals around her, their grunts, their smells, like a gargantuan serpent winding its way across the savanna. They then slowly broke into a trot and gradually into a run. She too found herself running, running faster and faster,

"Yes, yes, my love, I am coming back, coming back to you......." She cried. Her head spinning in ecstacy. Suddenly, she stumbled, she felt the parched earth come up and strike her forehead, and all at once the sound of thundering hoofs engulfed her, like the pounding of a tsunami. At first the pains were excruciating, but little by little she became numbed by the constant trampling's, she seemed to be falling into an endless-feeling-less abyss and eventually total darkness closed in about her.

When F. Farrell could not find her in the van, he knew instinctively that she must have followed the migrating herds. He thought, I should have known she was going to do this, dear Lord, will I ever find her? How can I inform her husband, I do not even know her name. Quickly, he started up the van to try and catch up to her before it was too late. By the time he came close to the stragglers of the herds, the others were well away, he searched on the ground for any signs – blood, clothing, shoes, but could find no evidence that she had been among them:

She had "Gone to Earth."

Two Minutes

Like nervous sheep, we were ushered into the examination hall – our Final Exams – the end of our present innocent life, and either the end also of our next one, or the beginning of that New Life. Silently we took our places, each individual at one of those typical Desk-seats common in all institutes of higher learning. Each of these seats were an "island unto itself" separated by isles and spaces to hinder even the cleverest of cheaters. As we sat down, the invigilator, Mother John Frances, announced in a menacing stage whisper,

"Please be seated. NO TALKING, NO WHISPERING, certainly NO EATING, NO SMOKING, and absolutely no looking over your neighbors' blue books."

The she came around, shuffling quietly in her nun's long black robe (we girls used to call it penguin's garb), and placed an examination paper within each Blue-Book-the ubiquitous examination answer booklet on the desk of each of those already nervous students. Then she continued in her dramatic whisper.

"DO NOT OPEN YOUR BLUE BOOKS NOR TOUCH YOUR EXAM PAPERS until I give you the word," then looking around piercing the poor victims with her dagger-like sky blue eyes, she sudden shouted, "NOW!"

The students were totally startled and intimidated, and for a second no one seemed to know what to do, then a great shuffle of papers went through the Hall, followed by dead silence, the Examination had begun. The shuffles were followed by incessant scratches of pen on paper, and the occasional sighs, faux coughs and noses blown needlessly. We immediately began to remember, recall and perhaps even to reinvent all that we had learnt in these past four years.

After about ten minutes, when things began to settle down, we suddenly noticed James Sprangle get up from his seat, walk up to Mother John Frances' desk to hand over his blue book. Mother looked up at James, nodded and pointed to the top right corner of her desk. He placed his Blue- Book there, held his head high, as if to disguise his own complacency, he turned around and gave the rest of us a cursive look as if to say, "You poor sods," and sauntered out of the room.

We returned to our own tasks, hoping we will do better than good old James, who probably new nothing and will get a well-deserved Zero for his efforts. After nearly three hours, the quiet and scratches were interrupted by secret swearing and expletives, and several of the students went up to the desk to hand in their own Blue-Books. Suddenly, the menacing whisper from Mother said,

"TWO MINUTE LADIES and GENTLEMEN!"

We quickly rushed to put the finishing touches to our answers. Exactly two minutes later a loud exclamation emanated from the table in the front of the hall: "Stop writing, pens down, NOW!" We all jumped in our seats and clattered our pens down, many dropping them on the floor.

"Starting from the first row on my right, come up and hand your Blue- Books and place them on the top right of my desk." Mother John Frances announced.

At this time, I quickly took a glance at the last sentence of the last question; "If you have read All the questions, you may hand in your Blue- Book now, and leave. You will automatically get an 'A.'"

I could have screamed, dug the 'proverbial hole' and buried myself. It was a total humiliation. Needless to say, James was the only student who passed with an 'A.'

About the Author

Pu-Chin Waide was born in Anhwei, China, amid the Sino-Japanese/W-WII era. In 1946, she relocated with her parents to India, where she spent her formative years. She completed her education at Loreto Convent, Darjeeling. Following high school, her parents sent her to UC Berkeley in the USA for further studies. It was there that she encountered Bevan Waide, a charming distraction who would become her husband. After tying the knot, Bevan joined the IRRD, and they established their home in Washington DC, raising a daughter and a curly-headed boy.

In 1969, they were posted to Dar-es-Salaam, Tanzania, on behalf of the Bank. However, in 1973, Bevan decided it was time to return to England. It was in Newcastle-upon-Tyne that Pu-Chin resumed her higher education. Unfortunately, in 1976, Bevan Waide was summoned back to the World Bank headquarters, prompting another relocation.

Once their children embarked on their own journeys, Pu-Chin and Bevan found themselves with an empty nest. Pu-Chin transitioned from full-time motherhood and homemaking to exploring various endeavors, such as 'design and build additions to houses, acupuncture, and pottery. Yet, she remained connected to her artistic pursuits, always keeping pencil and paper close. Maintaining a diary throughout her life, she penned short stories for her own enjoyment. Eventually, she published her father's memoirs after years of contemplation.

During a period of confinement at home following major surgeries, Pu-Chin, feeling both bored and irritable, decided to compile her short stories into small books. The first one titled "Fantasies, Imaginings, and Memories," followed by "Fantasies from Memories." These stories aim to bring laughter to readers' faces and, hopefully, music to their souls.